CW00340729

RONALD DUNN
FAITH
THAT WILL
NOT FAIL

Marshall Pickering

This is for
KAYE
who never stopped
believing

Marshall Morgan and Scott
Marshall Pickering
3 Beggarwood Lane, Basingstoke, Hants RG23 7LP, UK

Copyright © 1984 by Ronald Dunn
Originally published in the USA in 1984 by Tyndale House
First published in the UK in 1986 by Marshall Morgan and Scott
Publications Ltd
Part of the Marshall Pickering Holdings Group
A subsidiary of the Zondervan Corporation

Unless otherwise indicated, all biblical quotations are from the *New American Standard Bible*, copyright 1973, by the Lockman Foundation. Biblical quotations identified by KJV are from the *King James Version* of the Bible.

ISBN 0 7208 0687 9

Printed and bound in Great Britain by Anchor Brendon Ltd,
Tiptree, Essex

CONTENTS

The author wishes to acknowledge the following publications and publishers for materials quoted in this book:

All of Grace by C. H. Spurgeon. Copyright 1978 by Moody Press.

The Biblical Doctrine of Heaven by Wilbur M. Smith. Copyright 1968 by Moody Press.

Does God Still Guide? by J. Sidlow Baxter. Copyright 1968 by the Zondervan Corporation.

The Epistle of James by C. Leslie Mitton. Copyright 1966 by William B. Eerdmans Publishing Company.

The Epistle of St. Paul to the Galatians by J. B. Lightfoot. Copyright 1962 by the Zondervan Corporation.

The Epistle to the Romans by A. C. Headlam and William Sanday. Copyright 1901 by Charles Scribner's Sons.

The Epistle to the Romans, Volume II by John Murray. Copyright 1965 by William B. Eerdmans Publishing Company.

Evangelism in a Tangled World by Wayne McDill. Copyright 1976 by Broadman Press.

The Exploration of Faith by R. E. O. White. Copyright 1969 by Moody Press.

An Expository Dictionary of New Testament Words by W. E. Vine. Copyright 1940 by Fleming H. Revell Company.

Kneeling We Triumph by Edwin and Lillian Harvey. Copyright 1974 by Moody Press.

The Law of Faith by Norman Grubb. Copyright 1947 by the Christian Literature Crusade.

Let's Live by Curtis C. Mitchell. Copyright 1975 by Fleming H. Revell Company.

A Linguistic Key to the Greek New Testament, Volume II by Fritz Rienecker. Copyright 1980 by the Zondervan Corporation.

My Utmost for His Highest by Oswald Chambers. Copyright 1935 by Dodd, Mead & Company, Inc.

The New American Standard Bible. Copyright 1960, 1962, 1963, 1968, 1971, 1972, 1973, 1975, 1977 by the Lockman Foundation.

The New Testament in the Language of the People by Charles B. Williams. Copyright 1937, 1966 by Edith S. Williams. Moody Press.

The New Testament in Modern English, rev. ed., J. B. Phillips, trans. Copyright 1958, 1960, 1972 by J. B. Phillips. Macmillan Publishing Co., Inc.

New Testament Words by William Barclay. Copyright 1976 by Westminster Press.

The Path of Prayer by Samuel Chadwick. Copyright 1931 by Hodder & Stoughton, London.

A Pocket Lexicon to the Greek New Testament by Alexander Souter. Copyright 1956 by Oxford University Press.

Prayer Power Unlimited by J. Oswald Sanders. Copyright 1977 by Moody Press.

Revival in Romans by Walter K. Price. Copyright 1962 by the Zondervan Corporation.

INTRODUCTION

by George Duncan

It was in the year 1977 that I first met and heard Ronald Dunn
when we were both sharing in the ministry of the Gulf Coast
Convention in Houston, Texas. My immediate re-action was
that this man must be invited to preach at the great Keswick
Convention in England attended by some 8,000 Christians from
all over the world, and also at the Filey Convention held then
at Filey in Yorkshire and attended by some 7,000 Christians.
So it happened that Ronald Dunn was introduced to the British
Christian world. Straightaway he won his way into the hearts
of all who heard him and he has been invited regularly to return!
I was impressed with the clarity of his preaching, it was truly
scriptural and balanced, there was a warmth and penetrating
insight into the needs of the human heart, there was a delightful,
but not overdone sense of humour, and always there was a
challenge to the individual to be obedient to the truth of God.
The subject of this book is one that lies at the very heart of
the Christian's life day by day, we are not only saved by faith,
but we are to live and walk by faith, we serve by faith and in
that great 'Westminster Abbey' chapter in the Epistle to the
Hebrew Christian, the basis of all the effort and achievements
of the great men and women of God was 'by faith'. And yet
it is a word that many find difficult to understand and to
apply. In this book Ronald Dunn will have much to say that
I am sure will be of immense help to all.

George B. Duncan
Sussex 1984

9

PROLOGUE
All That Believes Is Not Faith

"If you had had enough faith," a friend tells a young widow, "your husband would not have died."

A husband and father of four quits his job in order to "live by faith." Church members must take food into the home to prevent his family from going hungry.

A twenty-year-old son dies suddenly, and his grief-stricken parents are told that if they were truly trusting the Lord they would rejoice rather than mourn, and "be thankful in everything."

A husband and wife contribute $2,000 to their church's mission campaign. When the check bounces, they explain with embarrassment that they wrote it by faith, believing God would miraculously add that amount to their account.

A minister falls ill with a treatable and curable sickness, but refuses medical help because he believes God will heal him by faith alone. While friends kneel around his bed to claim his healing, he dies.

These are a few of the recent encounters I have had with "faith." It's enough to give faith a bad name.

Is this what the Bible means when it says, "The just shall live by faith," and "Without faith it is impossible to please Him"?

Right now faith is enjoying renewed popularity; one could almost call it a faith awakening. On religious telecasts, in Christian publications, and from pulpits the power of faith is being preached and praised. Ordinary believers, resigned to casting a wistful eye toward the privileged land of faith, suddenly see it within their reach: they too can have a miracle and cause miracles to happen in the lives of others. Many are claiming to have faith, and many claims for faith are being made. Promises made in the name of faith range from the routine to the ridiculous, from "God wants you well," to, "Everyone can own a Cadillac." One evangelist recently announced that in his meetings God would fill teeth with gold and silver—the fillings being in the form of a cross.

But all that believes is not faith, and much of that being called faith today is not faith at all. All of which points to the sobering fact that it is easy to confuse counterfeit faith with the real thing.

Any day now someone is going to sue God for breach of promise—and considering our present addiction to litigation, I'm surprised it hasn't already happened. At the least, someone is bound to organize a consumer protection agency to protect the public from false advertising in religion.

Some words are like drapes that have faded from long exposure to the sun. Frequent use has drained the color from their meaning until they are no longer recognizable. Such words need, from time to time, to be reexamined to insure that their use is consistent with their meaning. And faith is a word dangerously close to fading. As Paul Tillich suggested, the word faith itself must be healed before it can be used to heal people.[1]

Many well-meaning Christians confuse the key of faith with counterfeit keys, keys that bear a remarkable similarity to faith but are actually look-alike replicas. Often what they judge to be faith is in fact presumption, or wishful thinking, or selfish desire, or some form of positive thinking. And when these bogus keys fail to open the doors of God's promises, some conclude that they are not of the "chosen few" and abandon any hope of living the life of faith.

But real faith never fails to open the door; it always achieves its goal. The question, then, is what is true faith? And how do we tell the difference between the true and the false?

A few years ago I met a man whose son worked for the Treasury Department. He told me he asked his son how the government trained the employees to spot counterfeit money. "I expected my son to say they studied the techniques of known counterfeiters, samples of phony money, and so forth," he said. But his son told him they learned to spot the counterfeit by studying real currency. "We get to know the real thing," he told his father, "so well, so thoroughly, that it's easy to spot the phony."

And that is what this book is all about—we want to study the real thing, to get to know it so well, so thoroughly, that we will be saved from deception and be able to master the art of living by faith.

NOTES

1. Hans-Jurgen Hermisson and Eduard Lohse, *Faith* (trans., Douglas Stott), (Nashville: Abingdon, 1981), p. 7.

PART ONE
FAITH
EXAMINED

CHAPTER ONE
The House That Grace Built

Salvation is like a house built beside a broad and busy highway. Like everyone else, I was born on that highway and was spending my life following it to its destination. At first the trip had been exciting and almost effortless, the constant flow of the crowd carrying me along. But the farther down the road I got the more difficult things became; my original joy had dissipated and I noticed that my fellow travelers rarely laughed anymore and their occasional smiles seemed forced. The backpack I had been issued at the beginning of my journey had grown heavier each day and I was now permanently stooped from its weight. Worst of all, I had been overtaken lately by an unexplainable fear of reaching the end of the highway.

One day my attention was drawn suddenly to the side of the highway to a magnificently constructed house. Over its narrow front doors a sign silently announced in bold red letters:

"WHOSOEVER WILL MAY ENTER AND FIND REST."

I don't know how I knew it, but I realized that if I could reach the inside of this beautiful house I would be saved from the highway and its destination. Pushing my way through the mass of indifferent travelers, I broke clear of the crowd and ran up the steps to the front door. But it was locked. *Perhaps it's only stuck*, I thought, and tried again. It refused to open. I was confused. Why would someone put up a sign inviting people in and then lock the door to keep them out? Not knowing what else to do (I refused to return to the highway), I pounded on the door, shouted for someone on the inside to open it, and tried to pick the lock—but it was useless.

Suddenly a voice spoke my name and I spun around. It was the Builder of the House. He placed in my hand a key on which was carved one word: FAITH.

Turning back to the door, I inserted the key in the lock, twisted it, and heard a reassuring click. The door swung open and I stepped across the threshold. Immediately the backpack fell from my shoulders, my back began to straighten like a wilting flower reaching for the sunlight, and from deep within me my soul breathed a sign of relief as an extraordinary sense of peace and well-being wrapped itself around me.

The Builder of the House welcomed me to my new home, explaining that everything in the house was now mine to enjoy. This was the house that grace had built, and faith was the key.

Surveying my new surroundings, I saw that the House of Salvation was a house with many rooms and I was only in the foyer. Across the way was a door marked Answered Prayer. Next to it was another that said, Daily Victory, and next to it, Every Need Supplied. The row of doors, each promising some spiritual blessing, stretched endlessly throughout the house.

The discovery of these other rooms puzzled me, for I failed to mention that the foyer in which I stood was jammed with people. It seemed that everyone who entered the house stopped in the foyer, never advancing beyond it, as though the foyer were the entire building.

This was little better than the highway. Couldn't they see that there was more to the House of Salvation than the foyer? Surely the Builder intended every room to be occupied. Hadn't He said that everything in the house was ours to enjoy? I, for one, had no desire to spend my life standing in a foyer. This was my Father's house; I was His child, and all He possessed was mine.

I went to the door marked Answered Prayer, grabbed the knob, and twisted. It was locked. I went to the next door, and the next, and the next. All were locked. But this time I didn't try to pick the lock or knock the door down. I remembered my encounter with the front door and knew you had to have a key.

Although I had been in the house only a short time, I had somehow managed to accumulate a large number of keys. Rummaging through my collection, I selected one tagged Doing Your Best, and tried it. It didn't fit. Nor did the key of Religious Activity. The key of Sincerity proved useless. Next I tried the key of Tithing (I was getting desperate); but it was as powerless as the others. I was beginning to understand why the foyer was so crowded.

And then I heard a familiar voice. It was the Builder of the House. "Child," He said, "do you remember the key I gave you to enter My house?"

"Yes, I remember."

"What was it?"

"Why, it was the key of Faith," I answered.

"The key of Faith," He said, "is a master key that unlocks every door in the house.

That was the greatest discovery of my life. Faith is the master key of the Christian life. From start to finish, salvation is a "by grace through faith" operation. Everything we get in the Christian life we get by grace through faith. Grace makes it available and faith accepts it. Grace is God's hand giving; faith is man's hand receiving. Faith possesses what grace provides. Grace is God's part; faith is man's part. It is our positive response to God's gracious offer. Everything God demands of man can be summed up in one word: faith.

Faith is the grasping of Almighty power;
The hand of man laid on the arm of God;
The grand and blessed hour

In which things impossible to me
Become possible, O Lord, through Thee.

— Anna E. Hamilton

Faith is the identifying mark of the Christian. In early Christianity it was the primary word used to describe our relationship to God; we were called "believers" before we were called Christians. To believe is our chief duty and the fountain from which all other duties flow. "This is the work of God," said Jesus, "that you believe in Him whom He has sent" (John 6:29).

The Bible indicts unbelief as the supreme evil and the source of all other evils. It was unbelief that led Eve to succumb to the devil's tempting voice in the garden. Unbelief locked the doors of the Promised Land against Israel and sent her wandering in the desert for forty years. Men are lost, not because they lie and steal, but because they refuse to believe (John 3:18). Unbelief tied the hands of Jesus in His hometown and robbed many needy people of His gracious help.

THE JUST SHALL LIVE BY FAITH

Four times the Bible declares, "The just shall live by faith" (Habakkuk 2:4; Romans 1:17; Galatians 3:11; Hebrews 10:38, KJV). When God says the same thing four times I get the idea He is trying to tell us something. And He is. He is trying to tell us that "the just shall live by faith." Note the word *live*. Not only are we saved through faith; we *live* by faith. Salvation commences with faith and continues the same way; we live the life the way we entered it. Faith is the pediatrician as well as the obstetrician. To the Corinthians Paul said, "We walk by faith" (2 Corinthians 5:7), and his personal testimony is recorded in Galatians 2:20: "The life which I now live in the flesh I live by faith in the Son of God."

Success in the Christian life is measured by faith. Always the word of Jesus is, "*Be it to you* according to your faith"

(Matthew 9:29). All our failures are failures in faith.

It is by faith that we please God. "Without faith it is impossible to please Him" (Hebrews 11:6). The writer doesn't say without faith it is difficult to please God—it is impossible.

It is by faith that the things possible to God become possible to man. "With God all things are possible" (Matthew 19:26). "All things are possible to him who believes" (Mark 9:23).

It is by faith that we overcome the world. "And this is the victory that has overcome the world—our faith" (1 John 5:4).

It is by faith that we resist the devil. "But resist him [the devil], firm in your faith" (1 Peter 5:9).   .

It is by faith that we conquer the problems of life. "Truly I say to you, whoever says to this mountain, 'Be taken up and cast into the sea,' and does not doubt in his heart, but believes that what he says is going to happen, it shall be granted him" (Mark 11:23).

It is by faith that we are made secure. "Who are protected by the power of God through faith for a salvation ready to be revealed in the last time" (1 Peter 1:5). After predicting Peter's sifting by Satan, Jesus assured the imperiled disciple that He had already prayed for him, that "your faith may not fail" (Luke 22:32). Peter could survive the sifting if his courage and zeal failed—even if his love for Jesus failed; but not if his faith failed. His faith was crucial; if that went, everything was lost.

It is by faith that we receive all God has promised us. "And everything you ask in prayer, believing, you shall receive" (Matthew 21:22). James 1:6, 7 says, "But let him ask in faith without any doubting, for the one who doubts is like the surf of the sea driven and tossed by the wind. For let not that man expect that he will receive anything from the Lord." Faith is the channel through which all that God has promised becomes ours. Through faith the blessings promised become the blessings possessed. Listen to these exciting words from Hebrews:

And what more shall I say? For time will fail me if I tell of Gideon, Barak, Samson, Jephthah, of David and Samuel and

*the prophets, who by faith conquered kingdoms, performed
acts of righteousness, obtained promises, shut the mouths of
lions, quenched the power of fire, escaped the edge of the
sword, from weakness were made strong, became mighty in
war, put foreign armies to flight* (Hebrews 11:32–34).

Neither God nor His methods have changed since those
words were penned. There is no new way of obtaining the
promises; the law of the Christian life is still, "By faith."

WHAT IS IT?

The Greek word for faith, also translated *belief* and *trust*,
means "the leaning of the entire human personality upon God
or the Messiah in absolute trust and confidence in His power,
wisdom and goodness."[1] Contained in the word is the idea of
intellectual conviction. Faith, then, is primarily an activity of
the mind and the will. Contrary to popular notions, there is
little or no emotion involved in biblical faith. Having been
intellectually convinced and firmly persuaded, we commit ourselves totally to that of which we are convinced and persuaded.
In the case of biblical faith, the basis of the conviction and
commitment is God. And, as we will see in a later chapter,
the convincer and persuader is the Holy Spirit.

The word faith has three basic uses in the Bible.

1. *The faith:* The whole body of Christian truth; the total
revelation of God to man; the gospel message. This is its
meaning in 2 Timothy 4:7, where Paul says, "I have kept the
faith," and in Jude 3, ". . . contend earnestly for the faith."

2. *Faith:* The act of believing, trusting, relying upon God.
This is the most common use of the word and is the primary
concern of this book.

3. *Faithfulness:* The quality of trustworthiness and steadfastness. Paul's Colossian letter is addressed to "the faithful
brethren in Christ." Paul was placed in the ministry because
the Lord "considered me faithful" (1 Timothy 1:12). This
quality is the result of the act of faith. God is faithful and

trustworthy and we become like the God we trust. Lightfoot says that the Hebrew and Greek words for faith "hover between two meanings: *trustfulness*, the frame of mind which relies on another; and *trustworthiness*, the frame of mind which can be relied upon." He goes on to say that the one quality of heart carries the other with it, "so that they who are trustful are trusty also; they who have faith in God are steadfast and immovable in the path of duty."[2]

To summarize, faith is an *affirmation*. It is our "Amen" to all God has revealed about Himself. We accept as true the facts God has disclosed in His Word.

Faith is an *act*. Not only do we believe all God has said, we obey all He commands. Our conviction leads to action. Hebrews 11 makes it clear that to believe God is to obey Him.

Faith is an *attitude*. As a result of our conviction about God and our commitment to Him, we accept His blueprint for our lives and, day by day, live in total dependence upon Him. Living by faith means believing that God is actively interested and involved in our daily existence. It means looking to Him for wisdom, guidance, and strength. This is the *rest of faith*, resting in His sufficiency moment by moment.

And it is this attitude of faith, this *resting* in Him, that God desires most. This is the goal toward which everything He does is directed; it is the result of the affirmation and act of faith. In Mark 4:40, when Jesus rebuked the disciples for their little faith, He was actually saying, "Have you not yet come to a settled attitude of faith?" They had had plenty of evidence that Jesus was able and willing to protect them and provide their every need—more than enough to bring them to a "settled attitude of faith." "Jesus aims to lead the disciples to such an abiding attitude of trust that the apparently dangerous can be faced with calmness."[3]

WHAT IS HE LOOKING FOR?

When Jesus saw the faith of the centurion (Matthew 8:10), He said, "Truly I say to you, I have not found such great faith with anyone in Israel." Jesus was *looking* for faith. Throughout His earthly ministry He searched the hearts of men and women for faith. And when He returns He will still be looking for that faith, for He says in Luke 18:8, "When the Son of Man comes, will He find faith on the earth?"

Faith is the essential commodity in the Christian life. It is not optional equipment, not a luxury item. Without it there can be no true spiritual life. To those who believe, nothing is impossible. And to those who believe not, everything is impossible. Samuel Chadwick said it well when he wrote:

Faith is enough. Faith is all God asks. Faith is all Jesus asks: "Ye believe in God, believe also in me." When the ruler of the synagogue was told that his daughter was dead, Jesus steadied his faith, saying, "Fear not: only believe"; and when the distraught father of the demoniac boy cried out against his own despair, our Lord assured him that "all . . . things are possible to him that believeth." Without faith man can do nothing with God, and God can do nothing with man.[4]

NOTES

1. Alexander Souter, *A Pocket Lexicon to the Greek New Testament* (Oxford: Clarendon Press, 1956), p. 203.
2. J. B. Lightfoot, taken from *The Epistle of St. Paul to the Galatians* (Grand Rapids: Zondervan Publishing House, 1962), pp. 154, 155. Used by permission of The Zondervan Corporation.
3. Herbert Henry Wernecke, *"Faith" in the New Testament* (Grand Rapids: Zondervan Publishing House, 1934), p. 32.
4. Samuel Chadwick, *The Path of Prayer* (London: Hodder and Stoughton, 1931), p. 65.

CHAPTER TWO
The Real Thing

It wasn't until I started to pay for the few items I had dumped on the counter that I realized all I had was a hundred dollar bill. I was in Ft. Collins, Colorado, speaking at a conference on the campus of Colorado State University, and the only money I had with me was this hundred dollar bill.

With a clatter of bells and buzzes, the cash register announced the total of my purchase: $7.02. I nonchalantly laid the hundred dollar bill on the counter.

"Don't you have anything smaller?" the clerk asked.

"I'm sorry," I said. "That's the smallest thing I have." I saw no reason to tell him it was the *only* thing I had.

Now properly impressed, the clerk scooped up the bill and, grasping both ends in his hands and stretching the bill tight, held it up to the light. I knew what he was doing, of course. Checking to see that it was good.

Then he did something unexpected. Picking up a notepad, he began to rub the bill vigorously back and forth against the white paper. And right before my eyes, the white paper turned green. The ink was coming off that hundred dollar bill! The thing was counterfeit! Where in the world had I gotten that bill? I couldn't remember. Here I was, a stranger in town, buying a mere seven dollars' worth of stuff with a hundred dollar bill. A classic way to pass funny money. Who would believe I didn't know the thing was counterfeit? I could see the headlines: BAPTIST PREACHER BAGGED WITH BOGUS BILL.

While I was frantically trying to think of a plausible story, the clerk stopped his rubbing, looked up, and smiled. "Well, it's good," he said.

"It is!"

"Yep," he said, pointing to the green-stained paper. "The real thing always rubs off."

What a relief. And what a lesson. Because I was unfamiliar with the nature of genuine U.S. Treasury bills, I thought I had a phony bill. And that is one of the real problems facing Christians in this matter of faith. If we don't know the nature of genuine faith, we will be vulnerable to deception and disappointment.

The sales clerk, confronted with a hundred dollar bill from a stranger, knew how to test it, knew how to determine its authenticity.

Could we do the same with faith? Faced with something claiming to be faith, would we know how to prove or disprove its claim? In this chapter and the next, we want to learn how to identify true faith. We will look at three basic characteristics by which biblical faith can be identified. Two of these we will discuss in this chapter, and the third in the following chapter.

FAITH'S CREDENTIALS: ITS OBJECT

True faith is authenticated by its object. "Faith in *what?*" is the question. *Believe* is a transitive verb requiring an object. When I hear someone say, "Just have faith," or "Only believe," I want to ask, "Faith in *what?* Only believe *what?*" You must believe something or someone. Faith must have an object. To many people, the important thing is to believe— *what* you believe is secondary. They have the notion that there is something mystical, magical in the mere act of believing, a sort of holy *shazam* that transforms simple mortals into Captain Marvels. But the truth is, faith itself has no power. It is not faith that moves mountains, it is God. This is not to deny that the exercise of believing is psychologically uplifting; but, biblically speaking, faith, as a mere human activity, possesses no virtue, holds no merit, contains no power.

The power of faith lies in its object; faith is only as valid as its object. The crucial thing is not faith, but the object of faith. You can believe with all your heart and soul and mind until you turn blue—but if your faith is aimed at the wrong object, you're wasting your time.

What is the proper object of faith? Jesus identifies it in Mark 11:22: "Have faith in God." The object of faith is God. Jesus didn't tell His disciples to "have faith," but to "have faith in God." Our faith must be *in God*. It may seem beside the point to mention this because everyone knows it, right? We might be surprised to find that our faith is frequently placed in things other than God.

For example, one writer advises his readers to "have faith in faith." Sounds sensible, doesn't it? Almost sounds scriptural. But the Bible never tells us to put our faith in our faith. That is positive thinking, not biblical faith. I don't mean to criticize positive thinking, or possibility thinking, or a positive mental attitude, or any such philosophy. I don't like negative thinking and I think we would all be happier and healthier if we maintained a positive mental attitude. But positive thinking is not the same thing as biblical faith. Faith will give you a positive attitude; but a positive attitude is not necessarily faith.

I labor this point because we seem to have a tendency to put our faith in our faith. When suddenly we encounter a mountain blocking our path and know that only by faith can we overcome it, we whip out our faith, hoping it is big enough to do the job. We measure it, weigh it, size it up in every possible way. And more often than not, we arrive at the sad conclusion that our faith isn't big enough to handle the crisis. How many times have we lamented over the weakness of our faith, using it as an excuse for failure?

"If only I had more faith."

"My faith is so small."

"Pray for me that I'll have more faith."

But the fact is that almost everyone who came to Jesus for help brought along a faith that was weak and imperfect. And yet in spite of their weak faith, Jesus miraculously met their need. Remember when the disciples were crossing the sea and a storm threatened to sink the boat? Jesus was asleep and the disciples ran to Him, crying, "Teacher, do You not care that we are perishing?" (Mark 4:38). Jesus rebuked the raging sea, then rebuked the faithless disciples. He did still the storm, in spite of their weak faith. I wouldn't have been surprised had Jesus said, "If your faith was stronger I would calm the sea, but because your faith is so weak, I'm going to let the boat sink." After all, their faith wasn't strong enough to stop a ripple, much less subdue towering waves. What counted was not the size of their faith, but the sort—its quality rather than its quantity. Although their faith was almost nonexistent, it had the right object—Jesus. What little faith they were able to muster, they brought to Jesus. It was not faith in their faith that saved them; it was faith in Jesus.

Frankly, I don't have much faith in my faith; I'm too well acquainted with it. I agree with Spurgeon when he said:

Never make a Christ out of your faith, nor think of it as if it were the independent source of your salvation. Our life is found in "looking unto Jesus" (Heb. 12:2), not looking to our own faith. By faith all things become possible to us, yet the power is not in the faith but in the God upon whom faith relies. . . . The peace within the soul is not derived from the contemplation of our own faith, but it comes to us from Him who is our peace. . . . See, then, that the weakness of your faith will not destroy you. A trembling hand may receive a golden gift.[1]

"Faith in faith" is really faith in yourself, in your ability to think positively and maintain a positive mental attitude. This means our attention is concentrated upon ourselves rather

than upon Christ. We are looking at our faith when we should
be looking at Jesus.

The writer of Hebrews, after parading before our eyes the
mighty heroes of faith, says, "Fixing our eyes on Jesus, the
author and perfector of faith" (Hebrews 12:2). *Fixing our eyes*
is the translation of a Greek word that means literally, "looking
away from and unto." As great as these men and women of
faith were, our eyes are not to be fastened on them or their
faith, but upon Jesus. We must look away from everything
else, our faith included, and concentrate on Jesus alone. James
McConkey writes:

*True faith pays no attention whatever to itself. It centers all
its gaze upon Christ. . . . When Satan cannot beguile us in
any other way he gets us to scrutinizing our faith, instead of
looking unto Christ. . . . That faith is the strongest which pays
no attention to itself. . . . Nothing will quicker weaken faith
than the constant endeavor to discover it. It is like a child's
digging up a seed to see if it's growing. It is a curiosity which
brings disaster to the seed. . . . Therefore do not worry about
your faith. . . . Take care that you are depending upon Jesus
. . . and faith will take care of itself.*[2]

Don't look at your faith, look at Jesus. Instead of measuring
your faith, measure your God. Rather than evaluating a situation on the basis of your faith, evaluate it on the basis of
God's ability. Is God capable? Is He big enough to handle
your problems? Who needs to ask? Of course, He is. Then
commit the situation to Him and trust Him to handle it. That's
what faith is—resting on God's faithfulness.

"But," you say, "my faith is so weak." Yes, but your God
is so strong. Which are you going to trust—your weak faith
or your strong God?

A few years ago my family and some friends from our church
spent a few days' vacation in Colorado. It was early March
and winter still had an icy grip on everything. Near the place
we stayed were twelve little trout lakes covered with ice. One

day one of my friends suggested I walk across one of the frozen lakes, assuring me it was perfectly safe to do so since they ice-skated on the lakes all through the winter. I've lived in the South and Southwest all my life, and the lakes there don't freeze solidly enough (if they freeze at all) to support the weight of a child, much less that of an adult. I promptly relayed these critical facts to my friend and respectfully declined his gracious offer.

Laughing, he said, "Come on, Pastor. It's safe. And it may be your only chance to walk on the water."

I still wasn't crazy about the idea, but after more coaxing, I ventured out. Perhaps ventured "out" is stretching it. I inched my way out not more than a couple of yards from the shore because, unlike Peter, I doubted Jesus would reach out and save me if I began to sink. I kept a nervous eye on the shore and one on the ice, watching for cracks. And I tiptoed, because you weigh less when you tiptoe. You didn't know that?

Anyway, after a brief and nervous walk on the water, I scrambled back to the solid safety of the shore. I had little faith in the ice.

Later, as we drove back to our lodge, we passed another of the trout lakes and as I looked out the car window I saw a man sitting in the middle of the frozen lake. He was sitting on a wooden crate, hunched over a hole in the ice, fishing! I did a double take at that, feeling foolish as I recalled my timid excursion on the ice.

Now to the point: The man sitting in the middle of the frozen lake had great faith in the ice—right? I had almost no faith at all in the ice. Now which one of us was the safest? He with his great faith, or me with my little faith? Surely the man with the great faith was more secure? The fact is, the man with the great faith was no safer than I was with my little faith. Though my faith was practically nonexistent, I was just as safe as the fisherman who possessed great faith.

Why? It wasn't our faith that held us up. It was the ice. If it had been our faith supporting us, I would have sunk immediately. But I, with my little faith, was just as safe as the fisherman with his great faith.

What, then, is the advantage of having a great faith?

I'm glad you asked. Picture me on the ice: timid, nervous, afraid to venture out, constantly looking for cracks in the ice, fearing that at any moment the ice is going to betray me to the icy water beneath. Know any Christians like that? Timid, nervous, afraid to venture out on the Word of God, their eyes constantly searching for cracks in His promises, fearing that God may at any moment abandon them. There is no joy or excitement in their walk. That is the life of little faith.

Picture the fisherman: unafraid to step out on the ice, boldly venturing to the very middle, enjoying himself, resting his entire weight on the ice. You have seen a few Christians like that; they boldly step out on the promises of God, unafraid in the middle of His will, filled with joy and satisfaction, resting on the Word of God who cannot lie. That's the life of great faith.

As we drove past, I said, "I wonder where he got enough nerve to do that."

The driver answered immediately, "Oh, he lives around here. He knows the ice."

He knows the ice. And that is the difference between faith and no faith, weak faith and strong faith. The Psalmist said, "And those who know Thy name will put their trust in Thee" (Psalm 9:10). And in Daniel's prophecy we read, " . . . the people who know their God will display strength and take action" (Daniel 11:32).

True faith is authenticated by its object, and the only valid object is God. The secret of faith is knowing God; and the greater our knowledge of Him and His Word, the greater will be our faith.

AS GOOD AS HIS WORD

In saying that God is the sole object of faith, I include also His Word and His promises. Faith in God and faith in God's Word add up to the same thing. Behind a person's promise stands the person himself; and we believe his word only to the degree that we believe in him. You can't have faith in God's

Word without having faith in the God who spoke it. And if we trust Him we will surely believe what He says to us.

When God gave Abraham the promises concerning his seed, the Bible says, "Then he believed in the Lord" (Genesis 15:6). Abraham's faith in God's promise is described as faith in the Lord. And you remember Paul's stormy voyage to Rome. When all hope of survival was swept away by the rampaging sea, Paul stood in the midst of the terror-stricken passengers and declared that God had spoken to him through an angelic messenger, promising that "there shall be no loss of life among you, but only of the ship" (Acts 27:22). And then the apostle, planted firmly on the promise of God, said, "Therefore, keep up your courage, men, for I believe God, that it will turn out exactly as I have been told" (Acts 27:25). Behind the Word of God stood the character of God, and that was good enough for Paul. For him, faith in God and faith in His Word were the same.

G. D. Watson said, "Our limitless trust in God seems to satisfy Him as nothing else can do, because it corresponds with His eternal faithfulness, it honours His veracity, and is a constant silent worship of all His perfections."[3]

FAITH'S CREDENTIALS: ITS OBJECTIVE

Throughout this volume we will again and again hammer at this fact: genuine faith is born out of a knowledge of the will of God and exists only to fulfill that will. The objective of faith is the will of God. Faith is not a means of getting man's will done in heaven; it is the means of getting God's will done on earth. Faith does not put God at our beck and call; rather it puts us at His. It is for "official use only," and is operational only within the sphere of His will.

This is probably the hardest thing to learn about faith; and to learn it well, two things are necessary.

1. *We must accept the will of God as the best thing that can happen*. More than to accept it as the best thing, we need to believe, really believe, that it *is* the best thing that can

happen, for it is. And, I suppose, we have to take even this by faith. For there are times when, to our sight and senses, the will of God appears to be less than the best. I remember one trying experience in my life when I had no doubt that what I was doing was the will of God—yet it was one of the most painful times of my life. I told some friends, "I don't see how anything this miserable could be the will of God." But it was, and the misery was only temporary.

When Paul describes the will of God as "that which is good and acceptable and perfect" (Romans 12:2), he means that the will of God in and of itself is good. It is intrinsically good. Nothing needs to be added to it to make it good. In other words, it is not the will of God plus a good job that is good, or the will of God plus my prayers answered that is good, or the will of God plus my baby being healed that is good. It is not the will of God *plus* anything; the will of God is good alone, all by itself.

To believe that God loves us is to be delivered from the fear of what He might do to us or withhold from us, for "no good thing does He withhold from those who walk uprightly" (Psalm 84:11). Like our Lord, we must learn to say, "My food is to do the will of Him who sent Me" (John 4:34).

2. *We must let the Bible say what it wants to say.* By this I mean we must refuse to manipulate the Word of God and must let it speak for itself. I think I can best illustrate this with an incident that occurred several years ago. I was conducting a Bible conference in Houston, Texas, and a friend I had not seen in four or five years dropped by the church. He explained that he was just passing through and happened to see the advertisements for the meeting in the newspaper. As we visited I learned that he had come by some new beliefs since I had last seen him. One of them was the belief that all sickness was of the devil and that it was always God's will for everyone to be healed. He quoted Matthew 4:23: "And Jesus was going about in all Galilee, teaching in their synagogues, and proclaiming the gospel of the kingdom, and healing every kind of disease and every kind of sickness among the people." And

then he quoted 1 Peter 2:24: "And He Himself bore our sins in His body on the cross, that we might die to sin and live to righteousness; for by His wounds you were healed."

I didn't want to get into an argument about divine healing, but I did feel I should point out something to my friend. "When you get back to your room," I told him, "I'd like you to read those two passages again, and I think you will see that the verse in Matthew is speaking only of what Jesus did during His public ministry on earth. Nothing is said about Jesus continuing that ministry after ascending to heaven. And the verse in Peter—if you study the context, it's obvious that Peter is talking about spiritual healing from our sins, not physical healing."

He returned the next day and said, "Well, I did what you asked. And you were right about both those verses."

I felt good; I had a convert.

Then he said, "Now I've got to find some new verses."

See the point? He had already made up his mind what he believed and he had to find some verses to try to support it. That's why we fall prey to manipulating the Bible to make it say what we want it to say.

The bottom line of all this is, if I believe the will of God is always best, then I will be satisfied to let the Bible speak for itself.

The third identifying credential of real faith is its origin. This will be discussed in the following chapter.

NOTES

1. C. H. Spurgeon, *All of Grace* (Chicago: Moody Press, n.d.), p. 44.
2. James McConkey, *Give God a Chance* (Chicago: Moody Press, 1975), p. 19.
3. Edwin and Lillian Harvey, *Kneeling We Triumph* (Chicago: Moody Press, 1974), p. 37.

CHAPTER THREE
The Origin of Faith

Some time ago I received a letter from a man defending a questionable doctrinal position. He wrote: ''I don't know the Bible or theology, but I have faith.'' He seemed to be saying that whatever difficulties existed with his position were overcome by the fact that he had faith. The bottom line was not, ''What does the Bible say?'' but ''Do I have faith?''

I don't doubt for a minute that he had faith. We all do. But what kind of faith? Faith is standard equipment in human beings; it is native to our nature. We live by faith, exercising it a hundred different ways every day. We sit in a chair by faith, believing it will support our weight. When we board an airplane we are placing our faith in the plane and the pilot. Our doctor tells us we have a disease we've never heard of, writes a prescription we can't read for a medicine whose name we can't pronounce, which we take to a druggist we don't know, who gives us a bottle of liquid that tastes like poison which we take and go back for more—that's faith.

But we do not commit ourselves to Christ with the same kind of faith we use to sit in a chair. A chair we can measure with our physical senses; Christ we cannot. While God has given to every man the capacity to believe, biblical faith is more than simply transferring our natural faith to spiritual objects. Just as a man's spirit must be reborn before he can fellowship with God, and his mind renewed before he can think after God, so his capacity to believe must be quickened before he can have faith in God.

Natural faith and biblical faith operate the same way, but in different realms. Take, for example, an AM radio and an FM radio. They function in the same manner: you plug them in, turn on the switch, rotate the dial, and pick up a station. But you can't tune in an FM program with an AM radio. They operate the same way, but in different spheres. And natural faith cannot operate in the spiritual realm.

WHERE DOES FAITH COME FROM?

In the last chapter we discussed two of faith's credentials. Now we come to the third, the origin of faith. Faith's origin is revealed by Paul in Romans 10:17: "So faith comes from hearing, and hearing by the word of Christ."

Faith *comes*. If a man has faith (from this point on when I speak of faith, I mean biblical faith), it had to come to him from an outside source. It did not originate within himself. Unlike natural faith, biblical faith is not native to man. Natural faith is inherent in man; biblical faith is imparted by God. A person may be born with a silver spoon in his mouth, but never with the key of faith in his pocket.

We do not generate faith or work it up. Faith is not convincing ourselves that something is true. When someone says, "I just can't believe," he usually means he is unable to convince himself that a thing is so.

A few years ago I had a terrific battle with insomnia. After several months of sleepless nights I went to the doctor for a complete physical. When the tests were completed he told me there was nothing physically wrong with me. He even told me I was not overweight. This surprised me, because I thought I was.

"You're too short," he said. "According to this chart you should be seven feet three inches tall."

Not only did my doctor crack jokes, he also refused to prescribe sleeping pills. But he said there was something he could do to help. He wanted to teach me self-hypnosis. This way, he said, I could put myself to sleep whenever I wanted and would awaken without a drug hangover. To be honest, I was reluctant. Something about hypnosis disturbed me. The word conjured up the picture of a nightclub magician in tails and top hat making people cluck like chickens and bark like dogs. But he assured me it was absolutely safe and perfectly natural, and that he had had great success with it in many patients. So I agreed to the six weekly sessions he required.

It was a great disappointment. Not because it didn't work— it did. But it was so utterly simple. Thinking I was to be initiated into some deep, dark mysterious secret, I learned that self-hypnosis is nothing more than talking yourself into going to sleep. You concentrate on an object such as a grease spot on the wall or a dead fly caught in a window screen, and start telling yourself over and over that you are sleepy. After a while your mind begins to believe what you're telling it and, bingo, you're asleep. It's simply mind over mattress.

And to many Christians, faith is a form of self-hypnosis. They try to talk themselves into believing, sort of psyching themselves up to a point where they believe, and then they hurriedly pray "before it melts."

But faith is not generated by us; it is given by God. It originates with Him; He initiates faith and imparts it to us. In 2 Peter 1:1, it says, "Simon Peter, a bond-servant and apostle of Jesus Christ, to those who have received a faith of the same kind as ours." And in Ephesians 2:8, we read: "For by grace you have been saved through faith; and that not of yourselves, it is the gift of God." From start to finish, salvation is a work of God. Everything involved in the saving of an individual originates with God, even the faith to receive His grace. In Philippians 1:29, Paul writes, "For to you it has been granted for Christ's sake, not only to believe in Him, but also to suffer for His sake."

Our faith does not depend upon our ability to believe, but upon His ability to impart it to us.

I stated earlier that natural faith and biblical faith are different, that biblical faith is more than taking the same faith we exercise in daily living and applying it to spiritual things. No one can believe God unless God enables him. This is made clear by the words of Jesus to the unconverted Jews of His day.

But though He had performed so many signs before them, yet they were not believing in Him; that the word of Isaiah the prophet might be fulfilled, which he spoke, "LORD, WHO HAS BELIEVED OUR REPORT? AND TO WHOM HAS THE ARM OF THE LORD BEEN REVEALED?" For this cause they could not believe, for Isaiah said again, "HE HAS BLINDED THEIR EYES, AND HE HARDENED THEIR HEART; LEST THEY SEE WITH THEIR EYES, AND PERCEIVE WITH THEIR HEART, AND BE CONVERTED, AND I HEAL THEM" (John 12:37–40).

Here is a striking example of men who *could not believe* because God refused to enable them to believe.

A similar incident is recorded in John 8:47: "He who is of God hears the words of God; for this reason you do not hear them, because you are not of God." These people could hear what Jesus was saying; they had ears and a natural ability to hear. But one does not hear the voice of God with physical ears and natural ability. Unless God imparts the spiritual ability to hear His voice, one hears nothing but meaningless words. We do not hear God with natural ears, nor do we believe Him with natural faith.

THE CREDIT GOES TO GOD

The focus of our concern should not be upon our inability to believe, but upon God's ability to enable us to believe. When the conditions are right (we will discuss the conditions later in this chapter), God will impart to us all the faith we need to trust Him in a given situation. It is a fundamental tenet of grace that whatever God demands, God provides.

When my brother and I were small boys we would go to our father at Christmas time and ask for money so we could buy him a present. Dad would give us a few dollars and we would go to town and buy him a Christmas present with his own money. On Christmas morning under the tree would be a gift with a card that read: "To Dad from Barry and Ronnie." It didn't occur to me how presumptuous that was—buying my father a present with his own money and then acting as though the gift came from me. It didn't occur to me until my children came to me at Christmas time asking for money so they could buy me a present.

It is the same with the faith we bring to God. We are simply presenting to Him that which He has given us. This means that whenever God puts us in a situation that demands faith we can be assured that He will provide the faith He demands. And He will never demand more than He has provided.

In this way God gets all the credit for any faith we may have; and thus, "no flesh can glory in His presence."

HOW GOD IMPARTS FAITH

Faith comes by hearing, says Paul, and hearing by the word of Christ. The instrument God uses to impart faith is His word.

1. The External Word. One of the most common misconceptions about faith is that it is a substitute for knowledge. One dictionary defines faith as "believing without evidence." As one child put it: "Faith is believing things you're not sure of." When we are uncertain about a person or a fact then we must "take it on faith." In other words, faith takes up where facts leave off. This may be true of natural faith but not of biblical faith.

Biblical faith is founded on facts—facts found in the Word of God. Faith begins with a knowledge of God's Word, without which there can be no genuine faith. I've heard people say, "If you believe with all your heart, you will get what you want." But this kind of faith is based on our own desires or sense of need. It originates within ourselves and depends upon our own ability to believe; it is religious self-hypnosis. This is the kind of faith the man had who wrote, ''I don't know the Bible, but I have faith.'' To him faith was a substitute for knowledge, a compensation for ignorance. Some even brag about their ignorance and glory in it as though it were a requirement for faith. To them knowledge is a barrier to believing and faith is a leap into the dark.

But faith is a leap into the light, the light of God's Word. Without this light we cannot exercise faith in God. Reduced to its simplest form, faith is *man's positive response to divine revelation*. It is action based on knowledge. Dr. Curtis Mitchell says:

In order to exercise biblical faith you have to have facts from God. You must have a Word from God on the matter. Otherwise you have no basis for biblical faith. Faith is founded on the Word of God. If you don't have a Word from God on the matter, then you are not in a position to exercise faith.[1]

Hebrews 11:1 defines faith as ''the assurance of things hoped for, the conviction of things not seen.'' The phrase ''things hoped for'' can be confusing if we don't understand the biblical use of the word ''hope.'' To us *hope* implies uncertainty; it is a wishing, a maybe, a perhaps. But there is not a trace of uncertainty in the biblical word. In the Bible, hope is based on divine promises. It is a word of assurance that we will receive what God has promised. The only uncertainty associated with biblical hope is the time of its fulfillment. The ''things hoped for'' are the things God has promised. If God has not promised them, all the believing in the world will not obtain them.

To discover what God has promised we must go to His Word. Ignorance of or indifference to the Bible results in little or no faith. The instances of imperfect faith recorded in the Gospels were directly related to imperfect understanding of the divine revelation. Look, for example, at the feeding of the five thousand. After the multitude had eaten, Jesus commanded His disciples to gather up the remaining food, which amounted to twelve baskets full. When this was done, He told them to get into a boat and make their way to Bethsaida. He would join them later. And join them He did—walking on the water. When the disciples saw Him they thought it was a ghost and were terrified. Then followed Peter's brief walk on the water. When he began to sink he cried out in fear. The Lord grabbed him and said, "O you of little faith, why did you doubt?" (Matthew 14:31). Mark's account ends with this explanation of their faithless fear: "For they did not understand the lesson of the loaves; their minds were dull" (Mark 6:52, Williams Translation).[2]

Loaves? What did bread have to do with boats? What did the feeding of the five thousand have to do with walking on the water? Their failure to understand the miracle of the loaves affected their behavior in the boat. Remember that the disciples gathered up twelve baskets of divinely produced food—that's one basket full for each disciple. Then they immediately boarded the boat, taking the baskets of food with them. Each disciple had at his feet the tangible evidence of the power of Jesus to provide and preserve, a basket filled with miraculously baked loaves. But they failed "to gain any insight" from that miracle. The lesson of the loaves was that Jesus is quite able to handle any situation that might arise. It demonstrated His power over all creation and, even more important, His compassionate concern for His followers. But the disciples failed to understand.

Still later the disciples again had a problem with boats and bread. Isn't it strange how we keep stumbling over the same problems? But the Lord continues to give us the exam until we pass. This time Jesus and His disciples take a boat to the region of Magadan. When they arrive the disciples realize they have forgotten to bring bread. At the same moment they make their discovery, Jesus warns them of the leaven of the Pharisees and Sadducees. The disciples interpret His words as a rebuke for forgetting the bread.

*But Jesus, aware of this, said, "You men of little faith, why
do you discuss among yourselves because you have no bread?
Do you not yet understand or remember the five loaves of the
five thousand, and how many large baskets you took up? . . .
How is it that you do not understand that I did not speak to
you concerning bread . . . ?"* (Matthew 16:8, 9, 11).

Do you not yet understand? Their little faith was caused by
their lack of understanding. A person does not have little faith
because he has little willpower to believe, but because he has
little understanding of the Word and will of God. Our ability
to believe is measured by our understanding of the Lord and
His Word. The centurion in Matthew 8 had such great faith
that Jesus marveled at it; but the source of his great faith was
in his understanding of Jesus and His mission.

In his book, *Evangelism in a Tangled World*, Wayne McDill
writes:

*The strength or weakness of our faith is directly related to the
accuracy of our knowledge and understanding of the nature
and purpose of God. Our faith depends on knowing something
factual about God. . . . Faith, then, is not reaching out to the
unknown, unbelievable, unseen possibilities beyond our own
understanding. Faith is rather, in the biblical view, a response
on our part to a clear word from God.*[2]

2. The Internal Word. But faith requires more than an intellectual knowledge of the Word of God; for while we cannot
have faith without knowing the Bible, it's possible to know
the Bible without having faith. I know of a minister who
worries himself sick over every little problem that comes along.
One day as he was fretting and fussing over a minor difficulty,
one of his associates said, "Pastor, why don't you just turn
this over to the Lord and trust Him to handle it?" Unhinged,
the pastor said, "I've never learned to do that!" This wouldn't
merit mentioning were it not for the fact that I have heard this

man preach several times about living by faith. It is possible to be a Bible scholar and at the same time not realize what it means to trust God in everyday living.

The impartation of faith requires more than intellectual knowledge of the Word. Let's take another look at Romans 10:17: "So faith comes from hearing, and hearing by the word of Christ." We're going to have to drill through some grammatical rock to get to the water to understand Paul's meaning. Throughout the New Testament two different words are used for "the word of God." The most frequent is the familiar word *logos*, meaning the expression of a thought, a message, a discourse. When referring to the Word of God, it means the total revelation of God, all that God has spoken to man, the gospel message. For instance, Jesus is called the Word (*logos*) of God in John 1:1 because He is the full and complete revelation of God to man.

The other word is *rhema*. This is a spoken word, an utterance, the concrete expression of *logos*.[3] *Rhema* is someone speaking, uttering.

Logos is the Word; *rhema* is a word from the Word. *Logos* is the message; *rhema* is the message spoken. *Logos* is the content of the message; *rhema* is the communication of that message. In *logos* the emphasis is on substance; in *rhema* the emphasis is on sound. *Logos* is the entire Bible; *rhema* is a verse from the Bible.

Commenting on the phrase, "the sword of the Spirit, which is the word [*rhema*] of God," in Ephesians 6:17, W. E. Vine says:

The significance of rhema *(as distinct from* logos*) is exemplified in the injunction to take "the sword of the Spirit, which is the word of God," Eph. 6:17; here the reference is not to the whole Bible as such, but to the individual Scripture which the Holy Spirit brings to our remembrance for us in time of need, a prerequisite being the regular storing of the mind with Scripture.*[4]

The word Paul uses in Romans 10:17 is *rhema*. Some translations read "the message of Christ" and give the impression that Paul is referring to the message about Christ that the preacher delivers. If Paul had used *logos* there would be no doubt that he was referring to the message about Christ; but the use of *rhema* suggests something more.

In this context, *rhema* can be translated *utterance*: "and hearing by the utterance of Christ." I believe the reference is not to the preacher's message about Christ, but *the actual utterance of Christ Himself*. In this tenth chapter of Romans, Paul makes a careful distinction between preaching and hearing. There must be preaching, but it is not preaching that produces faith; it is hearing. And the hearing to which he refers is not the hearing of the preacher's message, but rather of the utterance of Christ—the voice of Christ speaking through the message the preacher delivers. A person may hear clearly the preacher's utterance about Christ; but unless he also hears the accompanying utterance of Christ to his heart, there will be no faith.

This harmonizes with what Paul says in verse 14 of this same chapter. The King James Version reads, "How then shall they call on him in whom they have not believed? and how shall they believe in him of whom they have not heard? and how shall they hear without a preacher?"

The phrase, "how shall they believe in him of whom they have not heard?" is more accurately translated in the New American Standard Bible as, "how shall they believe in Him whom [not *of* whom] they have not heard?" There is a great difference in hearing *about* or *of* someone and actually *hearing* someone. Dr. Curtis Vaughan says, "There is a close connection here between the proclaimed word and the presence of Christ."[5] Paul is saying that if men are to believe they must hear Christ Himself.

The thought that Christ Himself speaks to us is also brought out in Ephesians 2:17: "And He came and preached peace to you who were far away, and peace to those who were near."

And again in Ephesians 4:20, 21: "But you did not learn Christ in this way, if indeed you have heard Him and have been taught in Him, just as truth is in Jesus."

THE FACT BECOMES A FORCE

All this means that there must be a spiritual hearing as well as a physical hearing, a quickening of our spirit by His Spirit that enables us to perceive the voice of Christ speaking to us through His Word. Without this divine quickening we will hear the words of the preacher but not the Word of God and, thus, be unable to act in faith on what we have heard. We may know what the Bible teaches about trusting Christ but we will have to confess, "I've never learned to do that."

Before there can be faith, divine enlightenment and enablement are required. Speaking of the condition of the lost, Paul says in 2 Corinthians 4:4, "In whose case the god of this world has blinded the minds of the unbelieving, that they might not see the light of the gospel of the glory of Christ, who is the image of God." He goes on to say that it is God who shines the light into our eyes that we may believe. No man can create his own light nor remove the blindfold from his eyes. That is accomplished by God alone.

But this divine enlightenment is needed by Christians as well. For the Ephesian believers Paul prayed, "that the God of our Lord Jesus Christ . . . may give you a spirit of wisdom and of revelation in the knowledge of Him . . . that the eyes of your heart may be enlightened, so that you may know what is the hope of His calling." A divine revelation to their hearts was required before the Ephesians could know and appreciate what they had in Christ.

Faith requires a personal encounter with the living Christ. When the woman of Samaria who met Jesus at Jacob's well rushed back to town with the news that she had found the Messiah, the men of the city went to see for themselves. After their encounter with Christ they said to the woman, "It is no longer because of what you said that we believe, for we have heard for ourselves and know that this One is indeed the Savior of the world'' (John 4:42).

After the resurrection, the disciples found it difficult to believe the reports of Christ's resurrection. They were convinced only after a personal encounter with Him. It took the resurrected Christ to assure them that He was indeed alive.

Our relationship to Christ is more than intellectual—it is personal and spiritual. It is not enough to hear or read the Bible. Christ must do for us what He did for the two disciples on the road to Emmaus: "And beginning with Moses and with all the prophets, He explained to them the things concerning Himself in all the Scriptures" (Luke 24:27). The word translated "explained" means "to open completely." Verse 31 says, "And their eyes were opened and they recognized Him."

Doesn't that strike you as strange? These men had accompanied Jesus for three-and-a-half years and yet they did not recognize Him until "their eyes were opened." They saw Him with their natural eyes; but recognition and belief came only when Christ enabled them to see with their spiritual eyes. Later in the same chapter we find Jesus speaking to the disciples concerning the things written of Him in the Scriptures. Verse 45 states, "Then He opened their minds to understand the Scriptures."

All this is to say that it takes more than an intellectual understanding of the Bible to produce faith. Thomas Aquinas said, "It is God who causes faith in the believer by prompting his will and enlightening his intellect." The Holy Spirit must illumine what He has inspired. As we hear the Word of God, Christ speaks to us through His Spirit, making the Word real to our hearts. The Word comes alive; the fact becomes a force. It is as though, while we are listening to the preacher, Christ whispers "Amen" to our hearts, giving an inner confirmation to what we are hearing. Only then are we able to grasp with the strong arm of faith the promise of God and appropriate all His grace has made available.

HOW TO HEAR

While faith is initiated and imparted by God, man is responsible for believing and is held accountable for any lack of faith. If we believe, it is because God enabled us; but if we do not believe, it is our own fault.

Israel heard but did not believe. The fault was theirs alone and God held them liable for their unbelief. Why did they not believe? In Romans 10 Paul states that faith comes by hearing; then he immediately says that Israel heard but did not believe. If hearing produces faith, why didn't faith come to Israel when the nation heard? The explanation is given in verse 21, and in that explanation are found the human conditions necessary for hearing with faith.

"But as for Israel He says, 'ALL DAY LONG I HAVE STRETCHED OUT MY HANDS TO A DISOBEDIENT AND OBSTINATE PEOPLE.' "

Note the twofold description of Israel: disobedient and obstinate. "Disobedient" refers to more than a simple, isolated act of disobedience. It indicates a stubborn refusal to obey, an unwillingness to be persuaded. Israel had made up its mind to disbelieve and disobey before it heard what God had to say.

"Obstinate" means to contradict what is said, to speak against it, to debate it.

Hearing did not produce faith in Israel because the nation (1) had already decided to disobey before it heard; and (2) Israel argued and debated what it heard. Turning these two negatives into positive attitudes, we conclude that if we are to hear with faith there must be (1) a readiness to obey, and (2) a willingness to listen.

1. A Readiness to Obey. I have been a minister for over twenty-five years, and most of my preaching has been to juries. You know what a jury is—it is a group of people who come together to listen to some facts, then go off and think about it for awhile. Then if the facts seem right and reasonable, they do something about it. And that's the way most of us listen to the Word of God. But God will not commit Himself to us on that kind of proposition. The Word of God is not on trial.

The proper attitude for hearing with faith is one that says, "Lord, I don't know what You are going to say to me, but I commit myself to obey what You say even before You say it." It is signing a blank contract and allowing God to fill in the terms.

"But I can't do that," someone says. Why not? Are you afraid God will take advantage of you? Do you believe that once He has you in His clutches He will pull some dirty trick on you? Suppose my son said to me, "Dad, from now on I'm going to do everything you tell me to do, without arguing about it or asking why." What would my reaction be? Would I say to myself, "Now I've got this kid right where I want him. Now, what's the dirtiest, meanest, lowest thing I can do to him?" Of course not. And if I, being evil, know how to give good things to my son, how much more does my heavenly Father?

A readiness to obey is the expression of our confidence in a loving heavenly Father. But we cannot expect God to reveal Himself to us if our attitude is, "First, tell me what You want and then I'll decide whether to obey." We must preface our hearing of the Word of God with a commitment to obey even before we know what it is He asks of us. That is a readiness to obey.

2. *A Willingness to Listen*. This is the correct order, for if we have decided not to obey, we are not going to listen willingly. A disobedient spirit makes hearing the Word impossible. But if we have settled the matter of obedience, we are eager to hear what God says.

This willingness to listen is what James referred to when he said, "Receive with meekness the engrafted word" (James 1:21, KJV). Meekness is having a *teachable spirit*. It is the attitude of a pupil before his teacher. The finest piano teacher in the world cannot help a student who debates and argues with everything the teacher says. A willingness to listen is listening with a view to obeying. We do not listen in order to weigh and evaluate what is said; we do not listen in order to offer suggestions or alternatives. We listen to obey.

We hear what we are prepared to hear. I have often assumed God wasn't speaking, when the fact was I was not hearing. The trouble was in the receiver, not the transmitter. It is God's responsibility to speak; ours to hear. It is God's responsibility to impart faith; ours to receive it. And God will impart to us all the faith we need if we are in the right position to receive it. You can depend on God to do His part. Our concern must be focused on our part—preparing our hearts to hear and receive. To those who are ready to obey and are willing to listen, God will speak. And we will hear—with faith. ''Speak, Lord, for Thy servant heareth.''

NOTES

1. Curtis C. Mitchell, *Let's Live!* (Old Tappan, N.J.: Fleming H. Revell, 1975), p. 115.
2. Wayne McDill, *Evangelism in a Tangled World* (Nashville: Broadman Press, 1976), p. 87.
3. Alexander Souter, *A Pocket Lexicon to the Greek New Testament* (Oxford: Clarendon Press, 1956), p. 227.
4. W. E. Vine, *An Expository Dictionary of New Testament Words* (Old Tappan, N.J.: Fleming H. Revell, 1940), p. 230.
5. Curtis Vaughan and Bruce Corley, taken from *Romans, A Study Guide Commmentary* (Grand Rapids: Zondervan Publishing House, 1976), p. 120. Copyright © 1967 by The Zondervan Corporation. Used by permission.

46

CHAPTER FOUR
Miracle, Anyone?

I have good news for you. There's nothing wrong with you
that a miracle wouldn't cure.

Now, don't you feel better? And you thought you were a
hopeless case.

If you're like most people, you are probably thinking,
"That's exactly what it will take—a miracle. And it will be
a miracle if I get one."

That's the trouble with miracles—never one around when
you need it.

Don't be too sure. One may be closer than you think.

But then, you don't really expect a miracle, do you? I
thought not.

Well, you're in good company. The Lord Jesus had a disciple
just like you. His name was Peter. One day as Jesus and His
disciples journeyed from Bethany to Jerusalem, they came to
a fig tree. From a distance Jesus could see that the tree was
heavily laden with leaves; and since leaves on those particular
fig trees signaled fruit, He expected to find the tree loaded
with fruit. But as He drew near He saw that the tree was
barren. It was a hypocrite. By bearing leaves it was claiming
to be fruitful; but it was false advertising. As a result, Jesus

cursed it, saying, "May no one ever eat fruit from you again" (Mark 11:14). The next day as they returned to Bethany they passed the fig tree, now withered from the roots up. Peter, remembering what had happened the day before, was astonished and said to Jesus, "Rabbi, behold, the fig tree which You cursed has withered" (Mark 11:21).

To Peter's exclamation, Jesus calmly replied, "Have faith in God. Truly I say to you, whoever says to this mountain, 'Be taken up and cast into the sea,' and does not doubt in his heart, but believes that what he says is going to happen, it shall be granted him" (Mark 11:22, 23).

Jesus was saying, "Peter, don't be surprised at the simple withering of a fig tree. That's nothing compared to what can happen if you have faith in God. Why, if you know how to believe God, you can command a mountain to jump into the sea and it will obey you."

That this was Jesus' meaning is made clear by Matthew's account of the same incident: "And Jesus answered and said to them, 'Truly I say to you, if you have faith, and do not doubt, you shall not only do what was done to the fig tree, but even if you say to this mountain, "Be taken up and cast into the sea," it shall happen'" (Matthew 21:21).

What a fantastic promise! Miracles at our command, mountains at our disposal. I would have been satisfied at withering fig trees, wouldn't you? But moving mountains. . . . And this shouldn't surprise us as though it were uncommon. Rather, it should be the norm, the ordinary, the expected. And the condition for fulfilling the promise is as amazing as the promise itself: "Have faith in God."

But, someone may ask, wasn't this some sort of dispensational promise limited to the original disciples? Two facts lead me to believe this promise is both eternal and universal in its application. First, the words preceding the promise, "Truly I say to you," are found throughout the Gospels and constitute a formula Jesus employed when enunciating a timeless truth.

Second, the promise says "whoever." Nothing in the verse or its context warrants limiting it to the first-century disciples.

Consistency demands that we interpret this *whoever* as having the same timeless application as the *whoever* of John 3:16.

WHAT IS A MIRACLE?

You probably won't find this definition in a theological textbook, but in my opinion it is accurate. A miracle is *God doing what only God can do*. It is a happening beyond man's power to produce or prevent. It is God moving that which cannot be moved, building that which cannot be built, destroying that which cannot be destroyed. This sovereign act of the Almighty may at times be spectacular and sensational; or at other times it may appear so ordinary that we fail to recognize it as a miraculous work of God. We declare with the authority of our ignorance, "The day of miracles is past." But the discerning eye of faith sees the hand of God in the "natural" as well as in the supernatural.

There's no doubt about it—this promise would strain the faith of the strongest saint. Did Jesus say what He meant? Did He mean what He said? Is it possible, if we have enough faith, to cast a literal mountain of dirt, rocks, and trees into the sea? Could I, by the sheer power of faith, relocate Mt. Everest to the nearest ocean? Frankly, I don't think that is what Jesus had in mind. I think He meant something far greater!

Remember our definition of a miracle: God doing that which only God can do. Given enough time and equipment and dynamite, man can move a mountain into the sea. But we're talking about something only God can do. Furthermore, we have no record of either Jesus or any of His disciples doing such a thing. Casting a mountain into the sea would serve no redemptive purpose; and we must remember that Jesus was no side-show sensationalist. Everything He did had a redemptive purpose.

In the Bible mountains are used to symbolize barriers and hindrances. They represent immovable objects, insurmountable problems that block the path of God's people, making progress impossible. For instance, Isaiah the prophet speaks

of the time when the people will be released from their captivity
and return to their homeland. But standing between them and
their destination are mountains, towering barricades shouting
like Amalek, ''This is as far as you go.'' Speaking through
the prophet, God says, ''And I will make all My mountains a
road . . .'' (Isaiah 49:11). God promises to turn the mountains
into a freeway; in other words, the mountains will be cast into
the sea, leaving the path open and clear.

A mountain is anything that threatens to halt or hinder our
God-appointed journey. It is anything that prevents us from
doing what God has commanded, or becoming what God has
promised. Jesus is telling us that if we can believe, there is
nothing that can keep us from doing what God has commanded
us to do or becoming what God has saved us to be. And that,
dear friend, is good news.

AN AMAZING PROMISE: "ALL THINGS ARE POSSIBLE"

To the questioning father of the demon-possessed boy, Jesus
said, ''All things are possible to him who believes'' (Mark
9:23). Whatever obstacle stands between us and the will of
God can be uprooted by the command of faith. Just think of
it. There is nothing, absolutely nothing, that can keep us from
doing the will of God—if we believe.

Behind the will of God is thrown the power of God. When
God commands us to be or do something, He places at our
disposal all the resources of heaven. And faith is the key that
releases those resources into our situation. If I know God's
will in a given circumstance, I can be assured that He stands
ready to supply whatever is needed to accomplish that will.

EVERY COMMAND A PROMISE

God never asks us to do anything that we cannot do. With the
command comes the ability to obey. When Jesus stood before
the grave of Lazarus He gave him an impossible command.
''Lazarus, come forth,'' He ordered. But that is an impossible

command. If Lazarus could come forth he would have done it before now. The Lord is asking too much: Lazarus can't come forth. But he does. For when Jesus issues the command He also imparts at the same time the power to obey.

One day Jesus met a man with a withered arm. "Stretch forth thine hand," Jesus said. But that is what is wrong with a withered hand—you can't stretch it forth. Yet he did. With the command came the power to obey the command. That makes every command a promise. If God commands us to do something, we know it is in fact a promise that can be fulfilled. No wonder the apostle John said that His commands are not burdensome (1 John 5:3). Our part, then, is to discover where God is going, join Him, and command the mountains to get out of the way.

AN AGGRESSIVE, AUTHORITATIVE FAITH

This kind of faith launches an offensive attack against the mountains that oppose the will of God. Rather than a passive, arms-folded, "there's-nothing-we-can-do-about-it" attitude, it is a shout that crumbles the walls of Jericho like dead leaves. It splits the waters of the Red Sea so we can escape the counter-attack of the enemy and march on toward the Promised Land. It refuses to accept the status quo when "the status ain't nothing to quo about."

Several years ago I spoke at a men's retreat in the beautiful Colorado mountains. We were experiencing an unusually blessed time; it was obvious God was moving in an extraordinary way in the lives of the 300 men present. As the men crowded into the chapel on the last night for the final service, the wind suddenly began to blow fiercely and steadily. To the right of the speaker's platform was a door leading outside. Evidently the weatherstripping was loose, because the wind began to whip around and under the door, creating a deafening howl that drowned out every other sound in the small chapel.

To make matters worse, the chapel was not equipped with a sound system. And to make matters still worse, I have a voice that has never boomed in its life. If I had had a loudspeaker I still could not have been heard above the roar of the mountain wind.

As I sat there waiting to speak and making halfhearted efforts to be "thankful in everything," I remembered that the Lord had once been forced to deal with an unruly wind. He commanded it to be silent, I recalled. His promise in John 14:12 came to mind: "Truly, truly, I say to you, he who believes in Me, the works that I do shall he do also; and greater works than these shall he do; because I go to the Father." That promise began with *two* trulys, so I figured it must really be true. Suddenly I found myself praying, "Lord, you surely didn't bring me here to be upstaged by the wind. This is Your meeting; these are Your people. I am Your servant; and that is Your wind. So I'm asking You in the name of Jesus to muzzle the wind as Jesus did on the Sea of Galilee."

And then I did something I have never done before or since. Almost without thinking what I was doing, I began to speak to the wind (softly, you understand; it seemed best that no one overhear me carrying on a conversation with the wind), and I commanded it to be still in the name of Jesus.

It was time for me to speak. The man who was to introduce me was shaking his head in frustration and pleading with the audience (who couldn't hear what he was saying), to listen to me. As I moved to the platform the wind suddenly stopped. It was as though someone had thrown a switch. Quiet— blessed, beautiful quiet settled over the chapel. And during the entire time I spoke, not a howl, not even a whimper, came from the wind. The 300 men heard easily. I finished and sat down. Immediately the switch was thrown and the wind took up where it had left off. But the mountain had been cast into the sea and the will of God done.

A SURPRISING REQUIREMENT: "TO HIM WHO BELIEVES"

This kind of power, power to move mountains, is released only by faith. The father of the demon-possessed boy cried out to

Jesus, "If You can do anything . . ." to which Jesus replied, " 'If You can!' All things are possible to him who believes" (Mark 9:22, 23). The question is not, "Can God do it?" but, "Can I believe?" It is never a question of His ability but of our faith.

Let's take a closer look at the incident involving the boy and his father. Jesus, you remember, was on the Mount of Transfiguration with three of His disciples. The other nine waited in the valley below. While they waited, a father appeared with his son and asked them to deliver the boy from his tormented condition. It was not a far-fetched or surprising request, for since Jesus had bestowed upon them the power to cast out demons they had seen many such spirits flee at the mention of that name. But now something was wrong. In spite of all their efforts, they were powerless to free the boy.

When Jesus returned, the father reported the disciples' failure; and Jesus, taking charge of the situation, commanded the demon to leave the boy. Afterwards the puzzled disciples came to Jesus privately (I don't blame them for coming privately— they must have been terribly embarrassed by their public failure) and asked why they had been unable to deliver the boy. Why were they suddenly unable to do what Jesus plainly promised them they could do (Matthew 10:1)?

It was a good question, for them and for us. Does it ever bother you—this terrible discrepancy between what God says we are and what we really are? God has promised us power; yet we are weak. He has promised to supply all our needs; yet we are forced to beg at the world's back door for money to keep our religious machines running. He promised that sin would not have dominion over us; and yet we are being delivered again into bondage. He promised that we would reign in life through Christ; yet we live like slaves, imprisoned by the world, the flesh, and the devil. Isn't it time we got alone with Jesus and asked why?

.What is the answer? What reason did Jesus give? I was more than mildly shocked by the explanation put forth by a well-known theologian. Commenting on this incident in one of his books, he claimed that the gift to cast out demons bestowed upon the disciples by Jesus was a temporary one. The only thing wrong with that explanation is it is wrong. That was not the reason given by Jesus. He didn't say, "You know, men, I knew there was something I forgot to tell you. That was a temporary gift and it expired yesterday at noon."

Nor did He explain their failure by saying, "Well, fellows, demons are tougher than they used to be. Why, I remember the time when just a snap of the fingers would send them running for cover. But times have changed."

Forgive me if I sound irreverent. I don't intend to be; but some of the reasons we offer for our tragic impotence are just as irreverent—and just as wrong.

What *did* Jesus say? "Because of the littleness of your faith; for truly I say to you, if you have faith as a mustard seed, you shall say to this mountain, 'Move from here to there,' and it shall move; and nothing shall be impossible to you" (Matthew 17:20). In Mark's account Jesus answered, "This kind cannot come out by anything but prayer" (Mark 9:29). There is no real contradiction in the two answers, for prayer and faith are two sides of the same coin. Faith encourages us to pray and prayer is the true expression of our faith. (See Mark 11:23, 24.)

Jesus' answer is unmistakably clear—the secret of the disciples' failure was their lack of faith. No other reason is given, for no other reason exists. This calls to mind Matthew's comment concerning Jesus' ministry in His hometown of Nazareth: "And He did not do many miracles there because of their unbelief" (Matthew 13:58).

WHY FAITH?

Why this divine insistence upon faith? The answer, I believe, revolves around three words: *grace, glory*, and *guarantee*.

Grace. In Romans 4:16, Paul says, "For this reason it is by faith, that it might be in accordance with grace." Grace can operate only through faith; that is the only environment in which it can exist. To set aside faith is to make grace inaccessible. Since grace is God's unmerited favor toward man, the only way man can receive it is by faith. If it comes to him because of his goodness or his parentage or anything else, it ceases to be unmerited; thus it ceases to be grace. And that is why man has such a hard time with faith: it strikes a fatal blow to his pride. It is extremely difficult and downright traumatic for human nature to sing a song like, "Jesus paid it all; all to Him I owe." Old Adam would choke on such words.

We have this need to contribute something; our ego demands it and feeds upon it. But faith forces us to admit that the things we truly need are beyond our power to produce and that only God can provide them. Calvin said, "Faith brings a man empty to God, that he may be filled with the blessings of Christ." Faith puts man right where God wants him—in the place of total dependence.

Glory. Faith glorifies God and brings honor to His name. Faith is man's positive response to the revealed character of God. Unbelief, therefore, is an assault upon God's character and an insult to His integrity. To disbelieve God is to deny that He is what He says He is; it calls into question His wisdom and power and goodness. That is why Spurgeon said that "to trust in the Lord Jesus is the climax of virtue."

Guarantee. Again in Romans 4:16, Paul gives another clue as to why God demands faith: ". . . in order that the promise may be certain to all the descendants." That the promise may be certain to all; and such certainty is possible only on the basis of faith. If any basis other than faith is required, then some will be excluded. For regardless of how easy and simple you make the requirement, some will be unable to meet it. But anyone, everyone, can believe.

Walter K. Price quotes one of his college professors as saying, "The genius of Christianity lies in its method of accessibility, for it is both universal and democratic. Anyone can believe—from the president of the university to the garbage man!''[1] Christmas Evans used to say, ''I can take a man, tie him hand and foot, nail him in a barrel and shout through a knothole what he must do to be saved and he can do it!''[2]

WHAT IS YOUR MOUNTAIN?

Have you found yourself saying, ''If it wasn't for this circumstance, I could be what God wants me to be?'' Is there a specific something that is preventing you from fulfilling the will of God in your life? That is your mountain. And you can be certain you have one, for the Christian life is never unopposed. The Ship of Zion is a Man O' War, not a luxury liner. God expects us to face opposition from the world, the flesh, and the devil. But that unholy trinity and the mountains they pile up before us can be swept away by the weakest Christian who knows how to believe God.

NOTES

1. Walter K. Price, *Revival in Romans* (Grand Rapids: Zondervan Publishing House, 1962), p. 25.
2. *Ibid.*, p. 25.

CHAPTER FIVE
The Wizard of Is

The Christian lives in two worlds. He is resident of this present evil age and of the Age to Come. Though he is a citizen of this world, the Bible says his "citizenship is in heaven" (Philippians 3:20) and that already he is "seated . . . with Him in heavenly places, in Christ Jesus" (Ephesians 2:6). As a believer he has been delivered "out of this present evil age" (Galatians 1:4) and has "tasted . . . the powers of the age to come" (Hebrews 6:5). Eternal life is a present possession. The Christian lives simultaneously in the physical world and in the spiritual world, in the seen and in the unseen, in the present and in the future, on earth and in heaven.

This new age, the Age to Come, dawned with the coming of Jesus into the world. His message was, "The Age to Come *has* come!" and He demonstrated it by His power over death, disease, and the devil.

These two ages, the present evil age and the Age to Come, do not run in temporal succession but exist side by side. In other words, the Age to Come doesn't begin when this present evil age ends; it has already begun. It began 2000 years ago at Bethlehem. Somewhere in the future this present evil age will cease and only the new age continue; but for the present they are running on parallel tracks. While the kingdom of God will have a future visible manifestation, it has already arrived in the hearts of believers. We have already been delivered from "the domain of darkness, and transferred . . . to the kingdom of His beloved Son" (Colossians 1:13). As a pledge of this we have been given the Holy Spirit (Ephesians 1:14).

The Christian can live a heavenly life on earth! He has tasted the powers of the Age to Come (Hebrews 6:5). Now a "taste" isn't a seven-course meal, but it is just as real. The difference is in quantity, not in quality. And the quality of life that he will someday experience in heaven can be experienced right now on earth. Jesus taught us to pray for the will of God to be done on earth as it is presently being done in heaven (Matthew 6:10). "A prayer such as this, taught us by the Lord Jesus, certainly must be one that can be fulfilled. We *can* do the will of God on earth as it is in heaven, or the prayer is mockery."[1] This means that through the believer heaven can actually infiltrate earth.

If all this is true, and it is, why then do so many of us fail to experience this quality of life? There seems to be a great gulf fixed between what the Bible says we are and what we really are in daily experience. According to Paul, "God has blessed us with every spiritual blessing in the heavenly places in Christ" (Ephesians 1:3). And Peter informs us that "His divine power has granted to us everything pertaining to life and godliness" (2 Peter 1:3). We were meant to "live . . . like kings" in this life (Romans 5:17, Phillips), but the average Christian is a spiritual pauper. How can this be?

ABSOLUTE AND APPROPRIATED

We must recognize the difference between the believer's *position in Christ* and his experience of that position. Writing of the sanctification of the believer, Merrill F. Unger says:

It is at this point that confusion is interjected in the minds of so many believers. They fail to see that this is a positional truth—truth that applies to the mind and reckoning of God and concerns the eternal and unchangeable placement of the believer in Christ as the result of Christ's redemptive work on the cross.

This positional truth must be differentiated and yet related to experiential truth. The latter has to do with the believer's comprehending and appropriating positional truth by faith, thereby making it realizable in his actual experience. . . . Faith in our position of sainthood in Christ conveys the benefits of sainthood into our experience.[2]

Everything God has done for the Christian is *absolute* but must be *appropriated*. For example, the sacrificial death of Christ was *absolute* in that He died for every man. God's love in Christ was directed at the whole world (John 3:16); and John the Baptist declared Jesus to be the "Lamb of God who takes away the sin of the world" (John 1:29). In 1 John 2:2 we are told that Christ is "the propitiation [*satisfaction, covering*] for our sins; and not for ours only, but also for those of the whole world." But this does not mean that all are saved automatically. That absolute atonement must be appropriated by faith. The Bible says, "He who believes in Him is not judged; he who does not believe has been judged already, because he has not believed in the name of the only begotten Son of God" (John 3:18).

The Bible also states that the devil was defeated absolutely and completely by the death of Christ. In Hebrews 2:14 we read that Christ died "that through death He might render powerless him who had the power of death, that is, the devil." And John tells us that "the Son of God appeared for this purpose, that He might destroy the works of the devil" (1 John 3:8). The devil and all his cohorts were stripped of their power and disarmed by the cross of Christ (Colossians 2:15). Well, then, somebody ought to inform the devil of his defeat! He certainly doesn't behave like a conquered enemy. On the contrary, he goes about like a roaring lion, seeking someone to devour (1 Peter 5:8).

While the devil's defeat is *absolute*, it must be *appropriated*. It is our business to inform him in the name of Jesus that he is a defeated enemy; and we are told to "resist him, firm in your faith" (1 Peter 5:9). Because Satan has been conquered, James can say with confidence, "Resist the devil and he will flee from you" (James 4:7).

Another example of appropriating the absolute is found in Romans 6. In the first ten verses Paul establishes the fact that we have died with Christ. It is our identification with Christ in His death that frees us from a life of sin. That is our *position*. To make that position experiential, Paul tells us in verse 11: "Even so consider yourselves to be dead to sin, but alive to God in Christ Jesus." On this point Unger writes:

Saints can and do sin when they fail to know and depend on their position of sainthood. Many saints do not know their placement as saints (Rom. 6:1–10). Many who do know it do not believe it and thus constantly fail to convert its benefits into daily living (Rom. 6:11).[3]

The believer must recognize his position in Christ with all its attending privileges and by faith appropriate it in daily experience. Our experience will be in direct proportion to our appropriation.

Speaking of our position, let's go back to Philippians 3:20 where Paul says, "For our citizenship is in heaven." The word *citizenship* signifies a colony of foreigners who, though living in a foreign country, live by the laws of their own country and model their lives after their native home. Philippi was a Roman colony whose inhabitants, though not actually in Rome, lived as though they were. They dressed like Romans, talked like Romans, and even thought like Romans. Living in Philippi, they obeyed the laws of Rome. The meaning of Paul's statement is that since we are citizens of heaven we are to live according to the laws of heaven rather than the laws of earth.

We are doomed to failure if we try to live the heavenly (Christian) life according to the laws of this world. When Jesus rebuked Peter for his foolish remarks about avoiding the cross, He said, "This view of yours is not from God but from men" (Matthew 16:23, Williams). The apostle Philip tried to operate by the laws of earth when Jesus asked him what could be done about feeding the five thousand. Just as most of us would have done, Philip dug into his pocket, counted his money, and evaluated the situation on the basis of earthly laws: "Two hundred denarii worth of bread is not sufficient for them, for every one to receive a little" (John 6:7). Even Andrew fell into the trap; he said, "There is a lad here, who has five barley loaves, and two fish; but what are these for so many people?" (John 6:9).

Israel was sentenced to forty years in the wilderness because in their expectations they limited the power of God to the laws of earth. The spies reported that the land was filled with giants; and Israel, being mere grasshoppers, could not possibly defeat them. After all, anybody with any sense at all knows a grasshopper can't whip a giant. That is the law of common sense, drafted by the wisest of human minds.

Jesus made it clear that we are not to live by the principles of this world when, after rebuking Peter for using his sword in the garden, He told Pilate, "My kingdom is not of this world. If My kingdom were of this world, then My servants would be fighting, that I might not be delivered up to the Jews; but as it is, My kingdom is not of this realm" (John 18:36).

LIVING IN THE HEAVENLIES

God has blessed us with every spiritual blessing in Christ Jesus in the heavenly places (Ephesians 1:3). Notice the location of the blessings: *in the heavenlies*—the spiritual realm. That's where Christ is seated (Ephesians 1:20); that's where the believer lives (2:6); that's where the blessings are (1:3); that's where the action is (6:12). If these were the blessings of God in the "earthlies" they could be obtained by earthly means. But being located in the heavenlies, they can be acquired by heavenly means only. When the astronauts went to the moon and brought moon-rocks back to earth, they had to forsake the laws of earth and operate by the laws of the moon. And if we are to bring the blessings of God to earth we must likewise abandon earthly laws and live by the laws of heaven.

To put it another way, God has deposited the riches of heaven in our account, but unless we know how to write checks on that account we will spend our days in spiritual poverty.

So the big question is, *how?* How do we move heaven into earth? How do we make what is ours positionally ours experientially? How do we operate by the laws of heaven instead of the laws of earth?

The answer is *faith*. It is faith that appropriates the absolute and bridges the experience gap between what God says we are and what we really are.

Faith's part in this is stated in Hebrews 11:1, a key verse in the study of faith: "Now faith is the substance of things hoped for, the evidence of things not seen" (KJV). This is more than a definition of faith; it is a statement of faith's power and activity. This is what faith does.

As we saw in chapter four the "things hoped for" are the things promised but not yet received. The "things hoped for" embrace all the blessings and benefits of a citizen of heaven. The word *substance*, translated in the New American Standard Bible, *assurance*, is a very interesting Greek word. It can also be translated *confidence* or *guarantee*. Moulton and Milligan offer this definition:

Used in Greek for property, estate, land-agreement of sale. It stands for the whole body of documents bearing on the own-ership of a person's property, deposited in the archives and forming the evidence of ownership. . . . *And as this is the essential meaning in Heb. 11:1, we venture to suggest the translation "Faith is the* title-deed *of things hoped for."*[4]

All the things God has promised belong to me as a member of His kingdom family. They are mine; they are my inheritance; I own them. But before I can take possession of them in experience, I must prove ownership; I must produce the title. This refers to faith, the "title-deed of things hoped for." Faith enables me to possess my possessions.

And now let's look at the most strategic word in that verse. When a writer of the Greek language wanted to give special emphasis to a certain word, he did so by placing that word first in the sentence. Our English translations rarely reveal this emphasis because it would make for awkward reading, and so we often miss the emphasis the writer intended. Now, can you guess which word is placed emphatically at the beginning of this verse? The little word *is*. I've had a great time with this Wizard of *Is*.

The writer wanted to emphasize the fact that faith makes things a present reality. Faith *is* substance. It is the title-deed to all God has promised. Notice that the verse doesn't say, "Faith *brings* substance"; but rather, "faith *is* substance." Faith *is*, right now, at this very moment, the substance of things hoped for.

We often find ourselves praying something like this: "Lord, I have faith. Now when are you going to reward my faith and give me the substance?" But faith does not say, "I'm going to get it." Faith declares, "I have it." By faith, things future, the things we hope for, become a present reality. Faith reaches into the future, lays its hand on the hoped-for things, and gives them to us. Faith isn't hoping; faith is having. As J. Oswald Sanders says, "The function of faith is to turn God's promises into facts."[5]

THREE KINDS OF FAITH

We can divide faith into three categories. First, there is the kind of faith that says, "God can." We believe God can do anything. Nothing is too hard for Him, for with God all things are possible. But this is not the victorious faith of which the Bible speaks. It is passive and accomplishes nothing. Suppose you have a great problem; and upon hearing that God is able and anxious to deliver you, you say, "I believe God can solve my problem.'' Is it solved? No. We may believe God can solve the problem; but simply believing God *can* do it doesn't meet the need.

Then there is the faith that says, ''God will.'' This is better, but still short of the biblical ideal. You believe not only that God can solve your problem but that He will—someday. In the meantime you bite your nails, wring your hands, fret and fuss, and drive everyone within fifty miles crazy. There is more to real faith than believing God *will*.

The faith described in Hebrews 11:1 believes beyond God can and God will. It believes *God has*. This kind of faith declares it already done. Instead of waiting for God to create the provision, it steps into the provision already available. Isn't this what Jesus means in Mark 11:24? He says, ''Therefore I say unto you, What things soever ye desire, when ye pray, believe that ye receive them'' (KJV). The word *receive* is a Greek aorist tense which implies you receive it before you actually have it. Williams translates it like this: ''So I tell you, whenever you pray and ask for anything, have faith that it has been granted to you, and you will get it.'' Jesus literally is saying, ''Believe you have already got it and you'll get it.'' That is just another way of saying, ''Faith is substance.'' R. A. Torrey said that he worried for years over the grammar of that verse, until one day he stopped worrying about the grammar and started enjoying the promise.

Anyone can believe he has something *after* he receives it. That's walking by sight, not by faith. Biblical faith is believing you have something before you have it. You believe you have it because God says you have it and not because you see it in your hand.

WHICH CAME FIRST?

Most people believe God creates provision to meet our problem. When we run into a tough situation we plead with God to come through with a solution. But God doesn't create provisions to meet our problems. He creates problems (or, if you prefer, he *allows* problems) to meet His provisions.

Remember the man born blind, mentioned in John 9? The disciples asked Christ if the blind man or his parents were responsible for the problem. It was a perfectly natural question. But Jesus said, "It was neither that this man sinned, nor his parents; but it was in order that the works of God might be displayed in him" (John 9:3).

We find the same principle in the creation account. God made provision for every creature before He made the creatures. He made water, then fish; animals, then vegetation. Adam didn't have to hold his breath until God could create some air to breathe. But that's how we usually react to problems. We take a deep breath and hope God will hurry with a solution before we suffocate.

But God provides the supply before there is a need. Which came first, the last Adam or the first Adam? The last Adam. Which came first, sin or salvation? Paul tells us we were chosen in Christ before the foundation of the world (Ephesians 1:4). Revelation 13:8 speaks of Christ as the Lamb slain from the foundation of the world. Before there was a garden in Eden there was a cross on Calvary.

What does all this mean? It means that there exists no need in your life that God, by His grace, has not already met. He has already blessed us with every spiritual blessing and has already given us all things that pertain to life and godliness. But those provisions lie behind locked doors and only the key of faith can open them.

A good illustration of this is found in the experience of Joshua as he led the people into Canaan. God said to him, "Every place that the sole of your foot shall tread upon, that have I given unto you, as I said unto Moses" (Joshua 1:3, KJV).

Further on, in Joshua 2:24, we read, "And they said unto Joshua, Truly the Lord hath delivered into our hands all the land." With the city of Jericho it was the same. "And the

Lord said unto Joshua, See, I have given into thine hand Jericho'' (6:2). Every step Joshua took was on conquered ground. And today's believer, whether he knows it or not, walks on conquered ground.

This kind of faith was the key that unlocked the land of Canaan. Forty years earlier, Israel had marched to the doors of the Promised Land but had failed to enter because they would not believe God had already given it to them. They feared defeat in battle. But Joshua brought them in because he knew theirs was not a *victory to be achieved* but a *victory to be received*. The land was theirs already. Grace made it available and faith accepted it.

Another Wizard of Is appears in 1 John 5:4: ''And this is the victory that has overcome the world—our faith.'' For years I read that as though faith obtained the victory. I thought that if I believed long and hard enough, eventually the victory would be mine. But faith itself *is* the victory. The possession of faith constitutes victory.

Someone says, ''Do you mean to tell me that if I simply believe I have the victory, I *have* the victory?''

''That's right.''

''I don't believe it.''

''You don't have the victory either, do you?''

The phrase ''win the victory'' betrays an inadequate understanding of the Cross work of our Lord. By His death Jesus won every victory for us. The tense of the verb *overcome* indicates that it has already been done and remains done. Just think of it—every temptation you will face today was overcome by Jesus 2,000 years ago! You have only to step into the victory already secured. That's living in the luxury of Calvary. And we enter that victory the same way we entered salvation—by grace through faith. Grace obtains the victory; faith maintains the victory.

This positional victory becomes experiential when the Christian stands before his besetting, binding habit, a weakness that hounds him day after day, and declares, ''Lord Jesus, I thank You that on the cross You delivered me from this. It has already been conquered by Your blood, and by faith I now accept Your victory over it and thank You that it is done.''

Let's examine one more Wizard of Is: "My grace is sufficient for you" (2 Corinthians 12:9). I discovered this "is" while going through a titanic trial sometime back. I knew God's grace could be, would be, sufficient. But in the meantime I was under the circumstance rather than on top of it. I kept wondering when God's grace was going to be sufficient. What was taking God so long to fulfill His promise? And one day as I walked down the street, wallowing in self-pity, this verse leaped into my mind shouting, "*IS!* My grace *is* sufficient. Not will be, but *is*." For the first time I really saw the little word *is*. God's grace *is* sufficient; not can be or will be, but *is* right now, this very instant, sufficient. Standing in the middle of the street, I prayed, "Lord, I see it! I thank You that right now Your grace is making me sufficient for this trial." At that moment the verse came alive in my heart, the Holy Spirit made real what I had reckoned, and the grace of God became miraculously sufficient. When by faith I agreed with the Word of God, the Spirit made experiential what had before been only positional.

FROM PLEADING TO PRAISING

Faith is substance. God first began teaching me this truth a few years ago when I had my back to the wall financially. I needed five hundred dollars immediately and I saw no way to get it. I had exhausted (or so I thought) every possibility. At the same time I got sick. It was the good kind of sickness—not well enough to go to work, but not too sick that I couldn't enjoy staying home. I said, "This is of God. He has provided an opportunity for me to lock myself away and pray down the money." And that's what I did—almost. I knelt beside my bed and opened my Bible to Matthew 6:33: "But seek first His kingdom and His righteousness; and all these things shall be added to you." The ''all things'' referred to the physical necessities of life Jesus talked about in the preceding verses.

I knew God owned all the cattle on a thousand hills, that the silver and gold were His, and that it was up to me to pry (or pray—to me, they were the same) five hundred dollars out of His hands.

I prayed, "Lord, meet my need. Lord, meet my need. Lord, are You going to meet my need? Give me a sign." After praying like that for awhile I would read the verse over and over, trying to coax my bashful faith to the surface. Then I would renew my pleading and praying.

After about an hour of this the Lord seemed suddenly to say to me, "Read the verse again." I did. It hadn't changed. Then the Lord said something that shook me. "Don't you wish your banker had said that instead of Me?"

I thought about that, knowing He was correct. What if my banker had promised me that if I would concentrate on seeking God and doing His will, he would provide all my necessities? I knew I wouldn't be worrying about a mere five hundred dollars. Nor would I be begging and pleading with him to keep his promise. He was an honest man. I would simply inform him of my need and rest assured it would be supplied.

The Lord seemed to say, "Son, your problem is you have more faith in the word of a man than in the Word of God. All my "praying" had been unbelief in disguise. God, who is greater than man, cannot lie. And His resources far outweigh those of any bank. This God had promised that if I would simply seek first His kingdom and righteousness, all the material needs of my life would be met. Immediately I stopped pleading with God to meet my need and started praising Him for doing it. Within two days God provided the five hundred dollars. When I believed I already had it, I got it. Faith was substance.

There are heights of sweet communion that are
awaiting me,
There are ocean depths of mercy that are flowing
full and free;

There are precious pearls of promise that can
  ne'er be priced in gold,
There's a fulness in my Saviour that has
  never yet been told.

— J. Stuart Holden

NOTES

1. Wilbur M. Smith, *The Biblical Doctrine of Heaven* (Chicago: Moody Press, 1968), p. 144.
2. Merrill F. Unger, *What Demons Can Do to Saints* (Chicago: Moody Press, 1977), p. 31.
3. *Ibid*.
4. James Moulton and George Milligan, *The Vocabulary of the Greek Testament* (Grand Rapids: Eerdmans Publishing Company, 1930), p. 660.
5. J. Oswald Sanders, *Prayer Power Unlimited* (Chicago: Moody Press, 1977), p. 43.

CHAPTER SIX
Believing Is Seeing

A new phrase has surfaced recently in the scientific community. It is "parallel reality." This is the name given to the theory that our universe may not be the only one around; another may exist parallel to it. We are unaware of its existence (if it does exist) because we lack the perceptive equipment to see it. Physical reality comes to us through the physical senses; remove one of those senses and immediately part of the physical world becomes, so to speak, a parallel reality.

To a blind man, for instance, a rainbow could be called a parallel reality. It exists, but he lacks the capacity to perceive it and would not even know of its existence unless someone else had told him about it. But give him the sense of sight, and the rainbow moves into his world and becomes a part of his physical reality.

Take a man who has never seen or heard of television. He is unaware that the air around him is filled with television programs; they constitute a parallel reality. But plop him down in front of a TV set, turn it on, and suddenly the invisible becomes visible—the parallel reality becomes a physical reality. Interesting theory, isn't it? Some scientists even think this may explain UFOs!

Whether such a parallel reality exists, no one knows. It is just a theory. But I know of another parallel reality that does exist. There *is* an invisible world coexisting with our physical world. It is described in Colossians 1:16: "In Him [Christ] all things were created, both in the heavens and on earth, *visible and invisible*, whether thrones or dominions or rulers or authorities—all things have been created through Him and for Him" (emphasis added).

There exists an invisible world that is more real than our visible world. As a matter of fact, this invisible world is the *ultimate reality*. Hebrews 11:3 tells us that "the visible was made out of the invisible" (Moffatt). The explanation behind our universe is not physical but *spiritual*. This means that the ultimate reality is spiritual rather than physical, as is commonly supposed. What you *cannot* see is more real than what you can see!

This fact is brought out by Paul in 2 Corinthians. He says, "While we look not at the things which are seen, but at the things which are not seen; *for the things which are seen are temporal; but the things which are not seen are eternal*" (4:18, emphasis added). Paul has been describing the physical sufferings involved in his service for Christ, sufferings that would wilt and wither the strongest of men. But, says the apostle, "We do not lose heart." He is afflicted, but not crushed; hard-pressed, but never hemmed in; always perplexed, but never to the point of despair; always persecuted, but never deserted; knocked down, but not knocked out. And in the midst of these assaults he never loses heart, is never discouraged or driven to the point of throwing in the towel.

How does he withstand such pressure? He has discovered the secret of living in the unseen world, the world of eternity, the world of ultimate reality. And that secret is fixing his gaze upon and concentrating his attention upon (the literal meaning of the Greek word translated "look") the things that are not seen instead of the things that are seen.

Paul saw the invisible. With the apostle John, Paul knew that this present world is passing away—but the will of God, and those who do it, abide forever (1 John 2:17).

This was Moses' secret also. Consider the unbelievable sac-
rifices he made in order to obey God. He "refused to be called
the son of Pharaoh's daughter; choosing rather to suffer ill-
treatment with the people of God . . . considering the reproach
of Christ greater riches than the treasures of Egypt" (Hebrews
11:24–26). The reproaches of Christ or riches—how could he
make such an appraisal? Verse 27 provides the answer: "He
endured, as seeing Him who is unseen." If ultimate reality to
Moses had been the riches of Egypt he would have never left
the palace. But rather than look upon the things that were seen
(the pleasures and treasures of Egypt), he looked upon the
things that were not seen (the riches of Christ—thousands of
years before Christ was born!) and thus endured. Moses looked
beyond the visible to the invisible and saw the ultimate reality—God.

Remember Elisha's faint-hearted servant? One morning as
he prepared breakfast he glanced out the window and spotted
the king's chariots surrounding the house. Terrified, he cried
out to Elisha: "Alas, my master! What shall we do?" The
prophet calmly answered (I believe he may have stifled a
yawn), "Those who are with us are more than those who are
with them." Then he asked the Lord to raise the veil on the
unseen world. "And the Lord opened the servant's eyes, and
he saw; and behold, the mountain was full of horses and chariots of fire all around Elisha" (2 Kings 6:15–17).

What *caused* the young man's defeatist attitude? He looked
at the visible, thinking that what he saw with the eyes of flesh
was the ultimate reality, the final word. What *cured* him? With
the eyes of faith he looked beyond the visible to the invisible
and realized that the ultimate reality is not what is seen but
what is unseen. That was a case of parallel reality; the horses
and chariots of fire were there all the time, but he lacked the
perceptive apparatus to see them.

This ability to see and appreciate the things of the unseen
spiritual world is one of the basic differences between the saved
and the unsaved. The natural man, according to Paul, doesn't
accept spiritual things, "for they are foolishness to him, and
he cannot understand them, because they are spiritually ap-

praised'' (1 Corinthians 2:14). But the Christian, because he
has been equipped by the Spirit of God, knows ''the things
freely given to us by God'' (1 Corinthians 2:12).

WHAT YOU DON'T SEE IS WHAT YOU GET

Without a doubt, one of the most vital secrets of successful
Christian living is this ability to see the invisible. There exists,
unseen by natural eye and unperceived by natural senses, a
world of heavenly resources and divine power. The question
is, how do we enter that invisible realm?

Hebrews 11:1 tells us. ''Faith . . . is the evidence of things
not seen'' (KJV). Faith is the sixth sense that enables the
believer to move into the unseen and eternal world. The word
''evidence'' means *proof by demonstration*. In other words,
faith doesn't merely convince us that unseen things exist; it
brings them into the actual experience of our lives. It is evidence based on experience.

Faith is sight. Believing is seeing. If you want the key to
the famous faith chapter, Hebrews 11, read through it, re-
placing the phrase ''by faith'' with the words, *by seeing the
invisible*. The heroes of faith were men and women who could
see beyond the visible to the invisible and believed more in
what they could not see than in what they could see. Our
trouble is we believe that what we see is the final word on
any subject.

Believing is seeing means we believe what God has said
despite physical evidence to the contrary, and when there is
no physical evidence to support what He has said.

An incident in John 20 illustrates this. The disciples are
closeted in the upper room discussing in guarded tones the
curious events following their Master's death. Suddenly the
risen Christ appears, and the disciples see Him—all except the
absent Thomas. Later when the excited disciples tell Thomas
what happened, he scoffs and says, ''Unless I shall see in His
hands the imprint of the nails, and put my finger into the place
of the nails, and put my hand into His side, I will not believe''
(John-20:25). *Unless I see I will not believe.*

Eight days later Jesus reappears. This time Thomas is present and Jesus invites him to touch the nailprints and to put his hand into his side. Shocked into belief, Thomas falls to his knees and cries, "My Lord and my God!" Now observe how Jesus responded to Thomas' declaration of faith. "Jesus said to him, 'Because you have seen Me, have you believed? Blessed are they who did not see, and yet believed'" (John 20:29).

In effect, Jesus classified those who believe into two categories: those who say, "Seeing is believing"—"Unless I see I will not believe." That's seeing with the eyes of flesh.

Then there are those who say, "Believing is seeing"—"Blessed are they who did not see, and yet believed." That's seeing with the eyes of faith. And upon those Jesus pronounced a blessing. Surely Peter was referring to this when, years later, he wrote: "And though you have not seen Him, you love Him, and though you do not see Him now, but believe in Him, you greatly rejoice with joy inexpressible and full of glory" (1 Peter 1:8).

When Martha's faith faltered at the tomb of Lazarus, Jesus said, "Did I not say to you, if you believe, you will see the glory of God?" (John 11:40). Ruled as we are by our physical senses, we try to reverse the order and say, "First let me see the glory of God and then I'll believe." The old hymn about the cross says, "It was there by faith I received my sight." But if we sang it honestly we would probably say, "It was there by sight I received my faith." Like the taunting Jews around the cross, we say, "Let Him come down from the cross and then we will believe."

If we are to live by faith we must not allow our physical senses—what we see, taste, touch, smell, and hear—have the last word. We must move out of the sense realm into the Scripture realm. If our five senses tell us one thing and the Scriptures quite another, we must believe the Scriptures.

A church member told me he couldn't afford to tithe. He had figured and figured, but there was no possible way he could do it. "I've got it down in black and white," he said. "Figures don't lie." Well, neither does the Bible. And if God tells us to do something, there is a way to do it. God never commands us to do anything without enabling us to do it—if we are willing. This man's problem was not that he figured—there's nothing unspiritual about that. But he figured wrong; he figured without faith. In adding his figures, he forgot to include the good promises of God. His conclusion was based solely on things visible.

Faith is the evidence of things not seen. You may not *see* deliverance from a nagging habit; you may not *see* the answer to your prayers; you may not *see* the inexhaustible supplies of God provided to meet your need. Then how do you know they are there? If you can't see, touch, taste, smell, or hear them, what proof do you have that they exist? Faith is the proof. We believe such things exist because God's Word says they do. Our faith rests not on physical evidence but on scriptural revelation. We choose to believe the promises of a God who cannot lie.

SAVED FROM THE COMMOTION OF EMOTION

This understanding of faith frees us from the slavery of our feelings. The Bible, not our feelings, should determine our faith. Many Christians live by feeling instead of faith. Of course, there's nothing wrong with emotion; the capacity for emotional enjoyment is a gift from God. Let's face it—it feels good to feel good. But the abuse and misuse of emotion is a major problem of present-day Christianity and poses a real threat to spiritual maturity.

I've seen Christians kneel at an altar to commit themselves totally to Christ and claim the fullness of His Spirit, then rise from their knees with their finger on their pulse to see how they are doing. They want to hear angel wings flapping and feel goose bumps playing leapfrog up and down their spine. Then they will believe. But when we insist that God give additional confirmation beyond His Word, we void everything. We shouldn't ask God for additional proof about something He has stated plainly in His Word. Faith is its own fleece.

We tend to measure our spirituality by our emotional level. If we feel victorious then we must be victorious. We believe our prayers are getting through if we feel they are. Our feelings must say "Amen" to our faith. But emotions are fickle and fleeting and not to be trusted. As a gauge of spirituality they are about as reliable as a sundial at midnight. Emotion is but the echo of an experience and destined to fade into nothingness.

This slavery to emotion can take us even further astray. If no satisfying and supportive feeling presents itself we may try to create, or recreate, a mood that corresponds to the spiritual exercise we are engaged in. C. S. Lewis was wise to this ploy of the devil, and in his *Screwtape Letters* exposed it through a letter Screwtape writes to his nephew, Wormwood. The old veteran demon is instructing the rookie in the best ways to draw Christians away from the Lord. He writes:

Keep them watching their own minds and trying to produce feelings *there by action of their own wills. When they meant to ask Him for charity, let them, instead, start trying to manufacture charitable feelings for themselves and not notice that this is what they are doing. When they meant to pray for courage, let them really be trying to feel brave. When they say they are praying for forgiveness, let them be trying to feel forgiven. Teach them to estimate the value of each prayer by their success in producing the desired feeling; and never let them suspect how much success or failure of that kind depends on whether they are well or ill, fresh or tired, at the moment.*[1]

Trusting our feelings can be hazardous to our spiritual health. If our last prayer time was attended by ecstatic emotions, we may believe that unless the same feelings reappear the next time we pray, something is wrong with us. If we are engulfed with rapturous feelings while preaching, we are apt to think that that kind of feeling is heavenly evidence that we are preaching in the Spirit. And when next we stand to speak, if the remembered feeling is absent, we plunge into despair, thinking God has abandoned us or has withdrawn His Spirit.

At that precise moment, Satan seizes us by the throat of our guilt complex and shouts, "Aha! See, God has counted you unworthy. You may as well give up this work."

The Welsh revival that took place in the early years of this century was one of the most extraordinary works of God that modern history has witnessed. Evan Roberts, the unofficial leader of the revival, was greatly used of God and thus became a prime target for the deceptive tactics of the enemy. A close friend has preserved a report of two intimate experiences that bear upon this point.

The first of these occurred while Roberts was praying prior to a service in which he was to preach. As he prayed, the whole room was suffused with a dazzling glow and there seemed to be a creature of light standing close by. Roberts assumed it was an angel of the Lord. It was an exhilarating experience, and in subsequent times of prayer, he found himself expecting the phenomenon to be repeated. It never was.

The second experience came as he was sitting on the platform awaiting his time to preach. Suddenly there was thrust into his mind the number "fifty-seven." He was perplexed at his preoccupation with this figure and wondered what it meant. That night fifty-seven people trusted Christ as Savior. Again he was thrilled with the thought that he had been given a special revelation as to how many people would be converted. Subsequently he found himself waiting for similar information in other services. Like the experience with the brilliant light, it never happened again.

Later Evan Roberts came to the conviction that both these occurrences originated with the devil and were diversionary tactics designed to move him out of the spiritual realm into the sensual and sensational.

This does not mean that God will not allow us occasional emotional highs. But if we demand an emotional verification of His Word, He will probably withhold it, lest our faith rest on the feeling rather than the Word. Otherwise, when the feeling subsides, our faith will collapse.

I'm convinced that God wants to bring us to the place where

we trust in Him and Him alone, without the aid of emotional crutches. Jesus desires in us the same quality of faith He sought in Jairus. You will remember, this father had a daughter at the point of death. At his request, Jesus agreed to go to the man's house and heal the girl. On the way they met a woman who had been hemorrhaging for twelve years and Jesus took time to help her. By the time Jesus was ready to resume his journey to Jairus' house, one of the father's servants arrived with the news that the girl was dead. When Jesus heard that He said to Jairus, "Do not be afraid any longer; only believe, and she shall be made well" (Luke 8:50). Now Jesus had him right where He wanted him—and us.

As long as the girl was alive there was something visible, something tangible to cling to; there was something concrete to support his faith. But with the girl's death, the only thing he could cling to was the promise of Jesus. And that was enough. You can be sure that God will so work in our lives to bring us to the place where all we have to hang on to is the bare Word of God. And that is what faith is all about.

I do my hardest work before breakfast—getting up. Getting up is a lousy way to start the day. I never feel spiritual in the morning. And Sunday mornings are the worst. This is a real problem when you are a pastor with a congregation expecting you to deliver an inspiring and enthusiastic sermon. For years this troubled me to the point of despair. Saturday night I would go to bed feeling great—and spiritual. I would be excited about the coming Lord's Day and anxious to preach, convinced the Lord was going to bless in a mighty way. But during the night God would slip away and hide from me.

I know confession is good for the soul—but it can be bad for the reputation. Well, I have a confession to make. When I awoke on Sunday mornings, I felt so unspiritual, the last thing I wanted to do was preach. I spent most of the morning trying to figure out what I had done to cause God to abandon me. As silly as it seems now, this was very real then, and continued to cripple me until God taught me that my feelings have nothing whatsoever to do with my relationship to Him.

Our relationship is based on fact, not feeling. And the fact was, I was just as right with God when I awoke on Sunday morning as I had been when I went to sleep Saturday night. I may have lost the feeling, but that did not mean I had lost the victory.

If you are limping around on the crutches of feelings, throw them away and walk on the legs of faith.

SAVED FROM THE TREASON OF REASON

So much for emotion, but what about reason? Is faith contrary to reason? Am I not to think at all? Do reason and logic have a place in the life of faith?

These are good questions, for we are often made to think that faith and reason are antagonists. I heard a preacher say once that if God was to reveal truth to us, we must stop thinking. "If you thought it," he said, "God didn't reveal it." Not so. It is through our renewed mind that God transforms us and reveals His will to us (Romans 12:2).

Faith is not contrary to reason; it simply goes beyond it. Faith refuses to be limited by the boundaries of logic, and this may sometimes leave the impression that it is illogical.

When the twelve spies returned from their investigation of Canaan, ten of them said the land was filled with giants and it was not reasonable to think that grasshoppers could whip giants. And they were correct. Their conclusion was perfectly logical. But two of the spies, Joshua and Caleb, held a different opinion and believed the land could be won. They didn't ignore the existence of the giants, but neither did they ignore the faithfulness of their God who had promised them victory in battle. Faith doesn't hide from the facts.

The ten spies went no further than their reason could carry them; Joshua and Caleb went as far as reason could take them, then allowed faith to carry them the rest of the way. Faith transcends reason and goes beyond it.

Suppose you want to go to England. You get in your car

and drive to New York City and there you run into the Atlantic Ocean. As far as you know, there's no such thing as a transatlantic bridge, and you know your car won't float. You have gone as far as you can by that means of transportation. What do you do now, give up and turn back? No. You are not limited to one mode of travel. Instead of letting your car limit your trip, you board an airplane and fly the rest of the way. The plane doesn't deny or contradict your automobile; it rises above it; it transcends it.

The car carries you to a certain point; then the plane carries you beyond it. So it is with reason and faith. God intends us to use our heads. After all, He created, regenerated, and renewed our minds so we could think and reason as Christians should. But He doesn't mean for us to be limited by what seems reasonable to finite minds. Human reason, even regenerated human reason, has a limited range and can carry us so far. Then faith must take over. Faith continues and completes the trip reason begins.

While the ability to reason is God-given, it is nonetheless restricted to physical evidence and senses. And if we trust in reason alone, it will betray us. Reason cannot breathe the rarified air of the heavenlies.

Unlimited by reason and unaffected by feelings, faith enables us to penetrate the barrier between the visible and the invisible and reach into the heavenly world to lay hold of "things hoped for" and "things not seen."

PART TWO
FAITH
EXERCISED

CHAPTER SEVEN
Faith That Pleases God

What do you think of when you hear the word faith? I'll tell you what I think of. I think of *miracles*. The sound of the word calls forth visions of the dead being raised, mountains being cast into the sea, armies being put to flight, the laws of nature being suspended. All these have been attributed to the exercise of faith. But there is another miracle effected by faith, more miraculous than any of these—though it is seldom recognized and little appreciated. It is spoken of in Hebrews 11:5, 6:

By faith Enoch was taken up so that he should not see death; and he was not found because God took him up; for he obtained the witness that before his being taken up he was pleasing to God.

And without faith it is impossible to please Him, for he who comes to God must believe that He is, and that He is a rewarder of those who seek Him.

The noteworthy miracle in this story is not the detour Enoch took around death to get to heaven, but the fact that he was *pleasing to God.*

Faith is given, not that we may perform miracles, but that we may please God—which is the greatest miracle of all. The devil can work miracles, but he cannot please God.

Nothing greater can be said of us than that which was said of Enoch: "He was pleasing to God." And if this cannot be said of us, whatever else may be said is meaningless. For in this statement we find the purpose for which we were created and the standard by which our life is judged.

But the thing that captivates me most about Hebrews 11:6 is not the fact that we should be pleasing to God, but that we *can* be. Just think of it: fallen, sinful, selfish, finite people are able to please a thrice holy God, a God too pure even to look upon sin.

This is even more amazing when we remember how difficult it is to please *man*. Difficult? It's impossible. Not even God can please man. But, while we cannot please man with his low and lowering standards of right and wrong, and his incomplete knowledge of the real us, we can please a holy God who knows us through and through and from whom nothing can be hidden.

And this is accomplished by faith. The tense of the verb *please* indicates that apart from faith there is not a single moment when we are pleasing to God. Regardless of what we do, no matter how wonderful and sacrificial the act—apart from faith, it is unacceptable to God.

"Without faith it is impossible to please Him." But what kind of faith? "He who comes to God must believe." Believe what? That's what I like about the Bible—it never gives a mandate without giving the means of fulfilling it. We are told exactly, and very simply, what we must believe if we are to please God. The writer points to two things: if we are to please God we must believe that *God is real* and that He is a *Rewarder*.

GOD IS REAL

"He who comes to God must believe that He is." At first glance it appears the writer is saying that he who comes to

God must believe there is a God to come to; he must believe in the existence of God. But he surely means something more than this, because the people to whom he is writing are Christians; they already believe in the existence of God. To tell them they must believe there is a God would be unnecessary.

And what's more, to tell someone who wants to come to God that he must first believe there is a God to come to doesn't make sense. After all, he wouldn't be coming to God if He didn't believe there was a God, would he? That would be like asking someone how to get to New Orleans and being told, "First, you've got to believe there is a New Orleans."

No, I think he is referring to something more. Let me paraphrase the statement, adding a few words, and I think we will get at what the writer had in mind:

"He must believe that God *still* is, *even when it looks like He isn't.*"

The people the author is addressing were undergoing furious persecution. Persecution wasn't new to them; they had "endured a great conflict of sufferings" following their conversion to Christ some years before (Hebrews 10:32). But this time it was so fierce some were about to throw in the towel. The author was urging them to remain steadfast and faithful.

"We are not," he says, "of those who shrink back to destruction, but of those who have faith to the preserving of the soul" (Hebrews 10:39). And that's why Hebrews 11 was written—to remind these fellow believers that God had in times past proven Himself faithful in delivering His people, even when the prospects for deliverance were bleak. Remember, the writer cries, we are of those who have faith to the preserving of the soul. And that is the kind of faith that declares, "God is," even when it looks as though He isn't.

This is an affirmation of faith made in the face of overwhelming odds and contradictory circumstances.

At times it looks as if God isn't. Oswald Chambers speaks of those occasions when God withdraws "His conscious blessings" in order to teach us to walk by faith.[1] I doubt that God ever totally withdraws His blessings, but He may withdraw for a season those conscious or obvious blessings.

One of my favorite Old Testament characters is Gideon. In Judges 6 we find Israel suffering under the Midianite yoke of bondage. Gideon is beating out wheat at the winepress and hiding it from the Midianites, when suddenly an angel takes a seat under a nearby oak tree and says to Gideon, ''The Lord is with you, O valiant warrior'' (Judges 6:12).

Gideon probably jumped six feet off the ground when the angel spoke without warning. The angel may have been stretching it a bit by calling Gideon a ''valiant warrior.'' Do you remember what Gideon said in response to the angel's greeting? ''Oh my Lord, if the Lord is with us, why then has all this happened to us? And where are all His miracles which our fathers told us about. . . ? But now the Lord has abandoned us and given us into the hand of Midian'' (Judges 6:13).

If the Lord is with us, why then has all this happened to us? Gideon's theology was simple, not to say appealing: If God is with us, then nothing bad can happen and we will experience a miracle a day as proof of His presence.

Unfortunately, Gideon's miracle-a-day theology is still with us, stronger than ever. It is preached, mostly on TV by the Joy-boys, that if we are filled with the Spirit and trust the Lord we will always be healthy and wealthy, that we will have "all honey, no bees; no work, all ease."

On Thanksgiving Day, 1975, our eighteen-year-old son took his life. Earlier that year he had been diagnosed as having a mood disorder caused by a chemical imbalance in the blood. We knew there was danger of suicide, but we had taken all the medical precautions possible and had covered him with believing prayer. We had no doubt God would deliver him from this elusive and deceptive malady. When he died, it looked as though God had abandoned us and we felt like crying with Gideon, ''If the Lord is with us, why then has all this happened?'' But in spite of our traitorous thoughts and unwelcome feelings, we knew God was with us—that *God is*, even though at the time it looked like He wasn't.

Not long after Ron, Jr.'s, death I received a letter from some Christian friends in another state. They had heard of the tragedy and wanted to express their sympathy. But more than that, his death had unsettled their Gideon-shaped theology. They had a son about Ron's age and they said, "We know that you are a man of God and that you have dedicated your life to serve the Lord. We don't understand how *something like this could happen to you.*" They figured that somehow my commitment to Christ deserved special treatment from the Lord and earned me a certain immunity from disaster.

But the fact is, loving God doesn't guarantee a charmed life. No exception from dark days is promised those who trust in Christ. We remain a part of the human situation, and there are times when it looks like God *isn't*.

Habakkuk wrestled with a similar problem. In his day it was the Chaldeans who kept rewriting his theology. They had laid siege to the city and were threatening to annihilate the people. Judah was finished—unless God intervened. Habakkuk the prophet had been storming the citadel of heaven with passionate prayers, but so far God had done nothing. Finally, in despair, the prophet cried, "How long, O Lord, will I call for help, and Thou wilt not hear?" (Habakkuk 1:2). Why don't you do something, Lord? The Chaldeans are about to destroy us. That was his complaint. And then in the fifth verse, God answered, informing Habakkuk that He had done something but that the prophet wouldn't believe his ears. "For behold, I am raising up the Chaldeans" (Habakkuk 1:6). The very thing that made him think God was doing nothing was the very thing God was doing!

Occasionally someone will say to me, "God has really started working in my life." But God is always at work in our lives. He has never "started." What we really mean when we say that is, "God has finally started acting the way we expect Him to." But sometimes the very things that cause us to believe God is not at work constitute the very work God is at.

"AND OTHERS"

I love Hebrews 11, especially the last part beginning with verse 32, where the writer really flies. "And what more shall I say? For time will fail me if I tell of. . . ."

And then, like a typical preacher, he tells of what he doesn't have time to tell of:

Who by faith conquered kingdoms, performed acts of right-eousness, obtained promises, shut the mouths of lions, quenched the power of fire, escaped the edge of the sword, from weakness were made strong, became mighty in war, put foreign enemies to flight . . . (vv. 33, 34).

That's great isn't it? That's the kind of faith I want.
"And others were tortured—" (v. 35).
Oops. Must have misread that last bit. I'll try it again.
"And others were tortured."
That's what I was afraid of—I read it correctly the first time.

And others were tortured, not accepting their release . . . and others *experienced mockings and scourgings, yes, also chains and imprisonment. They were stoned, they were sawn in two, they were tempted, they were put to death with the sword; they went about in sheepskins, in goatskins; being destitute, af-flicted, ill-treated . . .* (Hebrews 11:35–37).

Is this the same faith spoken of in the earlier verses? I'm afraid so. The same faith that enabled some to escape death by the sword enabled others to endure death by the sword. Faith does not always wear the dazzling, silky purple of trium-phant deliverance—often it is garbed in the blood-caked rags of triumphant death. But to say one is inferior to the other is to reveal an awful ignorance of the ways of God. The same faith that enables some to escape, enables others to endure.

Vance Havner is a friend. For over fifty years this mountain-bred prophet has ministered to thousands through his preaching and writing. His wife, Sara, was one of the "and others." Of the more than thirty books he has written, none has helped more people than his account of Sara's illness and subsequent death. Let me quote from *Though I Walk Through the Valley.*

I had hoped for the miraculous healing of Sara and that we might bear a dramatic testimony to the direct intervention of God. I had a sermon ready. But it was not to be. . . . It did not please God to heal her. . . .

My disappointment was intense but sober thinking has changed my view. If a dramatic experience of healing had been ours it would have been sensational, but such experiences are rare and my listeners would have said, "That is wonderful but it happens only once in a while and is the exception that proves the rule. Most of us do not have such miracles. Our loved ones die, our hopes fade, and we need a word for those who walk the Valley with no happy ending to the story." I can see now that God denied me what I sought that I might bring a message to the multitude like myself whose prayers were not answered as hoped. . . .

So I preach and write for a host of fellow travelers through the Valley whose hopes, like mine, were not realized and whose deepest wish was not granted. If we can move through this Valley and come out in victory, we have found a greater blessing than if our personal wish had been fulfilled in some miraculous way.[2]

I have an idea that for most of us the problem is not that we lack sufficient faith to be healed—we lack sufficient faith to remain sick if that be God's will. It requires greater faith to endure than to escape, I imagine, and it is easier to believe that *God is* when it looks as though He is than to believe *He is* when it looks as though He isn't. And that is the kind of faith that pleases God.

GOD IS A REWARDER

"He who comes to God must believe . . . that He is a rewarder of those who seek Him" (Hebrews 11:6).

Let's break this down and examine each phrase separately.

He is a rewarder. The faith that pleases God believes that it is always worthwhile to seek the Lord, regardless of how fruitless it may appear to be. Those who set their hearts to honor Him by seeking Him with all their strength will not go unrewarded.

God is no man's debtor. This was brought home to the disciples in Mark 10. After sadly watching the rich young ruler walk away from eternal life, Jesus spoke of the difficulty of such rich people being saved. At that Peter said, "Behold, we have left everything and followed You" (Mark 10:28). Perhaps Peter expected Jesus to be impressed with this and praise them for their great sacrifice. But such was not the case. To Peter's words of self-congratulation, Jesus said, "Truly I say to you, there is no one who has left house or brothers or sisters or mother or father or children or farms, for My sake and for the gospel's sake, but that he shall receive a hundred times as much . . ." (Mark 10:29, 30).

Not long ago I talked with a woman who prayed every day for five years that a certain broken relationship within her family would be healed. "But in the end," she said, "it wasn't. God did not answer my prayers."

I thought: every day for five years, and then, not answered. I said, "Do you consider that those five years of praying were wasted?"

"Oh, no," she said. "I'm sorry if I gave that impression. In a way, those were the best five years of my life. I've never had a greater sense of God's presence and love."

She hesitated a moment, then said, "I hope you won't misunderstand what I'm about to say—but the five years of unanswered prayer and family problems—well, what God has done for me in that time is well worth it. If I could trade my unanswered prayers for what the Lord did for me, I wouldn't."

Those who seek. The King James Version reads, "that diligently seek him," which is better because the word translated *seek* is a compound verb, *seek out,* and "the preposition in compound always seems to denote that the seeker 'finds,' or at least exhausts his powers of seeking."[3] God is the Rewarder of those to whom His reward is worth the effort of exhausting themselves seeking. It is the attitude of the shepherd who goes out into the cold, damp night to search for one lost sheep *until he finds it*. It is the attitude of the woman who sweeps and searches her house for a lost coin *until she finds it*. It is the attitude of Jacob, wrestling with the angel, crying out, "I will not let you go until you bless me." No halfhearted search will uncover this treasure. God has a way of hiding Himself from the casual looker.

The faith that pleases God is the kind that believes His reward is worth whatever it takes to find it.

That seek Him. I think if *I* had written this verse I would have worded it differently. Something like, "He is a rewarder of those who seek the *reward*." Makes sense to me. After all, if what I need is the reward, shouldn't it be the reward I am seeking? If I need healing, shouldn't I seek healing? If financial help, shouldn't I seek finances? But the reward goes to those who seek not the reward, but the Rewarder.

SEEK FOR NOTHING MORE

I believe that the prayer-seeking of many believers goes unrewarded because they are seeking the wrong thing—the reward. They are seeking, not His face, but His hand. We are to seek Him and Him alone, because everything we need is in Him.

My favorite passage is Colossians 2:9, 10: "For in Him all the fullness of Deity dwells in bodily form, and in Him you have been made complete." What can be added to completeness? All the fullness of the Godhead dwells in Him; everything that is good and godly is in Him.

Think of it this way: He doesn't give peace, He *is* our Peace; He doesn't give knowledge, He is our knowledge; He doesn't give wisdom and righteousness and sanctification and redemption—He is all these things Himself (1 Corinthians 1:30).

Charles Wesley said it this way:

Thy gifts alone cannot suffice,
Except Thou be given,

For Thy presence makes my paradise,
And where Thou art is heaven.

Faith that pleases God loves Him for Himself and not for what it can get out of Him.

Several years ago, while I was conducting a conference in a Southern state, one of the church members asked me to come to his house and anoint him with oil, lay hands on him, and pray for his healing. As a Southern Baptist minister I don't get many requests like that. That night he told me of his problem. It had something to do with his hip joint, and although he had had several operations, he still could not walk without crutches. In the course of the conversation, he let me know that I was not the first preacher he had approached. As a matter of fact, he contacted every preacher who came through his city. And some of them were "biggies" in the healing ministry. That struck me as strange. If God chooses to heal us, surely it doesn't take Him thirty-seven preachers to do it. Something was not right. So I asked him a simple question.

"Why do you want to be healed?"

He seemed surprised that I would ask such an obvious question. Then he said, "It's like this. I belong to a prayer group—we meet every Monday night. And everyone in the group has a healing testimony except me. I'm the only member of the group who can't give a healing testimony."

As he talked further it became obvious that the others in his prayer group were growing suspicious of his spirituality because of his inability to get healed. Here was a brother who was seeking the reward instead of the Rewarder.

When I first started traveling I made it a point to bring something home for the children—a souvenir or toy—nothing expensive, just something to surprise them. Soon the highlight of Dad's homecoming was the opening of the suitcases, because somewhere beneath the soiled shirts and dirty socks lay a surprise. The kids hardly noticed me—they were too anxious to get to the suitcase. It got so bad that my wife tried to coach them on how to behave when they saw me.

"Now, kids," she would tell them, "act like you're glad to see Daddy."

But, bless their hearts, they were poor students of good manners when there were suitcases to be opened and treasures to be found. To tell the truth, at times it hurt just a bit—they seemed more interested in the cheap little trinkets I brought them than in the one who brought them—me, their loving father. But after all, they were just children.

The children are nearly grown now, and I still bring them gifts from distant and exotic places, like Tulsa and Omaha. I've noticed something, though. They actually seem happier to see *me* than what I have brought them. But after all, they are no longer children.

Once it was a blessing,
Now it is the Lord.
Once it was a feeling,
Now it is His Word.
Once His gifts I wanted,
Now the Giver own.
Once I sought for healing,
Now Himself alone.

— A. B. Simpson

Faith that pleases God believes that God is better than His best gifts.

SETTLE FOR NOTHING LESS

After making the pivotal statement of verse 6, the writer calls upon some of the patriarchs of the past to reinforce his word with their testimonies. A phrase in Abraham's testimony intrigues me. It's found in verse 9. Speaking of Abraham and his journey to the Promised Land, the writer says, "By faith he lived as an alien in the land of promise, as in a foreign land, dwelling in tents with Isaac and Jacob, fellow-heirs of

the same promise.'' The phrase I'm referring to is this one:
"He lived as an alien in the land of promise.'' When at long
last he finally reached the land of promise, the land God had
given him for an everlasting possession, Abraham lived as an
alien. He lived like a foreigner in his own country. And rather
than build permanent dwellings, he lived in tents, the mark of
a nomad, a transient. Why? Why didn't he build a solid house
and live as a citizen in his own land of promise?

The Scripture says that Abraham, when he was called,
obeyed and traveled under sealed orders to the place God gave
him. We naturally assume that when God called Abraham, it
was to the land that He had called him, and that's true. But I
believe there is a truer sense in which God always calls us to
Himself, that every call *from* God is a call *to* God. God Himself
is our inheritance, and the promises He makes are the means
He uses to draw us to Him.

At the risk of sounding irreverent, I believe the land was
the carrot that God held in front of Abraham to get him to
move out. What God had in mind for Abraham beyond the
land was a deeper knowledge of and closer fellowship with
Himself. And when Abraham finally arrived in the land of
promise, he had come to know God in a far deeper and richer
way—and the land meant little to him.

He was now "looking for a city which has foundations,
whose architect and builder is God" (Hebrews 11:10). No
wonder that he was able to unselfishly offer his nephew Lot
first choice of the land. Abraham had discovered something
better than the land—the Lord. Even in the land, his own land,
Abraham and the others confessed that they were strangers
and exiles on the earth. For "they desire a better country, that
is a heavenly one" (Hebrews 11:16).

That is where faith finds its rest, its promised land; not in
the transient blessings of this age, but in the very presence of
God. The faith that pleases God lives as an alien in the land
of promise.

Throughout Hebrews 11 runs the hint that no visible, material, or earthly fulfillment could satisfy their faith. Even in the land of promise they claimed to be strangers and exiles *in the earth*—not just in Egypt, but anywhere in the earth. And pilgrims and strangers they remained. Faith will do nothing but make you a stranger on this earth. If you are looking for anything else, forget it. Faith doesn't necessarily make life easier or more pleasant or more prosperous. The purpose of faith is to wean us from all else beside, till alone with Jesus we are satisfied.

Dr. R. E. O. White has a good word on this. He writes:

It is indeed characteristic of spiritual life that God's people are strangers and pilgrims on the earth, sojourners and travelers who have not *arrived. . . . It is the essential nature of pilgrim faith to continue seeking what it has not found, aiming for goals it has glimpsed but has not reached.*

There is a maturer faith than the faith that asks and gets; it is the faith that asks and goes without, patiently without complaint. . . . Mature faith does not live by answers to prayer, but by prayer.

Faith demands more than earth can give, and so must always be disappointed on earth. . . . Faith is a perpetually defeated thing which never accepts defeat. Because it knows, when it pauses to reflect, that its disappointment is but the measure of its hopes; its goal is too big to be attained just yet.[4]

The faith that pleases God believes that He is a Rewarder of those who seek Him. And what is that reward? It is Himself. To Abraham He said, ''Fear not, Abram; I am thy shield. and thy exceeding great reward'' (Genesis 15:1, KJV). God is both the Rewarder and the Reward.

My heart has no desire to stay where doubts
  arise and fears dismay;
Tho' some may dwell where these abound, my
  prayer, my aim is higher ground.

I want to live above the world, tho' Satan's
*   darts at me are hurled;*
For faith has caught the joyful sound, the
*   song of saints on higher ground.*

I want to scale the utmost height and catch
*   a gleam of glory bright;*
But still I'll pray till heav'n I've found,
*   "Lord, lead me on to higher ground."*

NOTES

1. Oswald Chambers, *My Utmost for His Highest* (New York: Dodd, Mead & Co., 1935), p. 305.
2. Vance Havner, from *Though I Walk Through the Valley* (Old Tappan: Fleming H. Revell, 1974), pp. 80, 81. Copyright © 1974 by Fleming H. Revell Company.
3. Fritz Rienecker, taken from *A Linguistic Key to the Greek New Testament*, Vol. II (Grand Rapids: Zondervan Publishing House, 1980), p. 361. Copyright © 1980 by The Zondervan Corporation. Used by permission.
4. R. E. O. White, *The Exploration of Faith* (Chicago: Moody Press, 1969), pp. 112–115.

CHAPTER EIGHT
Believing God—
A Case History

Once upon a time a first-grader, wanting to impress his parents, memorized part of the multiplication table. Standing at attention, he carefully recited, "Two times two equals four." Daddy beamed with pride. Mommy purred with delight. As they had suspected, their little darling was a genius. In the midst of their beaming and purring, the little boy asked, "What's a two?"

I suspect many Christians approach faith in the same way. While declaring, "I believe God," under their breath they are asking, "What's a believe?" The question rarely surfaces because everyone, of course, knows what it means to believe God, and no one wants to admit he does not know what everyone knows. And so they all stumble along the path of faith, suppressing the nagging fact that they don't really know how to exercise faith in God. For them there is a great gulf fixed between their claim to faith and their ability to believe God.

But to live the life of faith you must understand what is involved in believing God and "how to go about it."

In school the teacher could spend all day explaining how a certain math problem was solved, but until she actually worked out the problem on the blackboard, I couldn't grasp it. And it is the same with faith. We need to observe someone actually believing God. The Word must become flesh; the abstract must become concrete; and things invisible must be made visible. Truth is easier to grasp when clothed with flesh and blood, when theological propositions become historical persons. Faith requires this kind of incarnation. Of all the great biblical concepts, faith may well be the most abstract, the most intangible. It would help if we could watch someone go through the motions of believing God. We need to see someone do it.

And that is the object of this chapter. We are going to become apprentices in the work of faith. Our teacher is Abraham. He is our word made flesh. Biblically, the name of Abraham is synonymous with faith; he is the father of the faith and of the faithful. No other figure demonstrates so ideally what it means to believe God. His life is a monument to the declaration, "The just shall live by faith."

Romans 4 presents a clear picture of Abraham's faith. Here Paul shows step by step how Abraham exercised his faith in God and that it was reckoned to him as righteousness (4:22). In other words, everything Abraham needed, everything God demanded of him, was obtained by his faith. And then Paul says, "Now not for his sake only was it written, that 'IT WAS RECKONED TO HIM,' but for our sake also, to whom it will be reckoned" (4:23, 24). In preserving this account of Abraham's faith, God is not merely recording history, but presenting Abraham as the standard of faith for all believers. He is the representative man when it comes to faith. What was true of him is true of all those who believe as he believed. This fact is reinforced by the phrase in verse 16: ". . . those who are of the faith of Abraham, who is the father of us all." If we believe as Abraham believed, we will receive as Abraham received.

The passage describing Abraham is a classical presentation of faith.

Verse 16: "For this reason it is by faith, that it might be in accordance with grace, in order that the promise may be certain to all the descendants, not only to those who are of the Law, but also to those who are of the faith of Abraham, who is the father of us all."

Verse 17: "(As it is written, 'A FATHER OF MANY NATIONS HAVE I MADE YOU') in the sight of Him whom he believed, even God, who gives life to the dead and calls into being that which does not exist."

Verse 18: "In hope against hope he believed, in order that he might become a father of many nations, according to that which had been spoken, 'SO SHALL YOUR DESCENDANTS BE.'"

Verse 19: "And without becoming weak in faith he contemplated his own body, now as good as dead, since he was about a hundred years old, and the deadness of Sarah's womb."

Verse 20: "Yet, with respect to the promise of God, he did not waver in unbelief, but grew strong in faith, giving glory to God."

Verse 21: "And being fully assured that what He had promised, He was able also to perform."

Verse 22: "Therefore also IT WAS RECKONED TO HIM AS RIGHTEOUSNESS."

The act of faith has two sides: God's side and man's side, divine revelation and human response. Faith is man's positive response to God's revelation.

GOD'S SIDE — DIVINE REVELATION

All faith begins here. Before we can believe we must have a word from God. Examining Abraham's case we find a twofold revelation: of God's character and His will.

A Revelation of God's Character. Verse 17 describes God as the One "who gives life to the dead and calls into being that which does not exist." The character of God is the foundation of faith. You cannot trust someone you do not know. The Psalmist said, "And those who know Thy name will put their trust in Thee" (Psalm 9:10). It is God's character that inspires our faith; if we know His name (His revealed character) we will trust Him.

Everything in the Christian life depends upon an adequate understanding of who God is. There is God as He is and there is God as we conceive Him to be. We do not worship God as

He is but as we conceive Him to be. If our concept of God is wrong, our worship of Him will likewise be wrong. And an inadequate or inaccurate knowledge of God will result in a defective faith. As was pointed out in chapter four, those whom Jesus rebuked for their inferior faith had an inferior understanding of Jesus. The centurion's faith was superior because his knowledge of Jesus was superior. God's character inspires our faith, and before He asks us to trust Him, He reveals Himself (His character). His character defines and directs our trust.

An accurate knowledge of God is essential. Take the case of the Samaritan woman. As Jesus talked with her the conversation shifted to worship. She exposed her erroneous idea of worship when she said, "Our fathers worshiped in this mountain; and you people say that in Jerusalem is the place where men ought to worship" (John 4:20). Jesus corrected her by saying, "God is spirit; and those who worship Him must worship in spirit and truth" (John 4:24). Before He could set her straight on the nature of worship He first had to set her straight on the nature of God. God must be worshiped according to His nature. He is spirit; therefore, He must be worshiped in spirit. The nature of God determines the nature of worship.

The same principle is enunciated in 1 John. The apostle writes, he says, so that we may have fellowship with God; and, significantly, the first thing he discusses is the nature of God. "And this is the message we have heard from Him and announce to you, that God is light, and in Him there is no darkness at all" (1 John 1:5). In the next verse he says, "If we say that we have fellowship with Him and yet walk in the darkness, we lie and do not practice the truth; but if we walk in the light as He Himself is in the light, we have fellowship . . ." (1 John 1:6, 7). Our walk must correspond to His nature. God is light; therefore, we must walk in the light.

The life style of the believer is simply a response to the character of God. Peter writes, "But like the Holy One who called you, be holy yourselves also in all your behavior; be-

cause it is written, 'YOU SHALL BE HOLY, FOR I AM HOLY' "
(1 Peter 1:15, 16). Why should Christians be holy? Because
God is holy. No other reason is given. No other is needed.

Again the apostle John says, "God is love, and the one who
abides in love abides in God. . . . We love, because He first
loved us" (1 John 4:16, 19). In chapter two he tells us that
"the one who says he abides in Him ought himself to walk in
the same manner as He walked" (1 John 2:6).

And Christ said, "Therefore you are to be perfect, as your
heavenly Father is perfect" (Matthew 5:48).

Faith, then, is our response to the character of God. This
demands an ever-deepening knowledge of God. Augustine
prayed, "Grant me, Lord, to know and understand which is
first, to call on Thee or to praise Thee? And, again, to know
Thee or to call on Thee. For who can call on Thee, not knowing
Thee? For he that knoweth Thee not may call on Thee as other
than Thou art."

Spurgeon said, "The proper study of the Christian is the
Godhead. The highest science, the loftiest speculation, the
mightiest philosophy, which can ever engage the attention of
a child of God, is the name, the nature, the person, the work,
the doings, and the existence of the great God whom he calls
his Father."

Paul wrote to the Philippians: "I count all things to be loss
in view of the surpassing value of knowing Christ Jesus my
Lord, for whom I have suffered the loss of all things . . . that
I may know Him" (Philippians 3:8, 10).

THE REVELATION MATCHES THE NEED

To Abraham, God revealed Himself as the One who "gives
life to the dead and calls into being that which does not exist."
Why did God reveal these particular attributes of His character?
The answer lies in that for which Abraham had to believe God.
God promised him two things: one, he and Sarah would have
a son and; two, Abraham would become the father of many
nations. But there was a slight problem. Sarah's womb was

"dead," and Abraham, being a hundred years old, was as good as dead. For them to produce a son would be like bringing life out of death. And, in the light of his physical infirmity, to call Abraham a father of many nations was to speak of something that did not exist.

Was it possible to believe such a thing could happen? What would Abraham base his faith on? The nature of God! Resurrection and creation are two of God's specialties. Do you see it? The revelation of God's character corresponded with His promise. God gave to Abraham a staggering promise and at the same time gave him a revelation that would enable him to believe the promise. God made known to Abraham that part of His character that would inspire and enable Abraham to believe. The revelation matched the faith required. That's why I say that faith is based on the character of God; it is the human response to the divine revelation.

This principle is seen in Joshua's experience of faith. Faced with the herculean task of conquering Jericho, Joshua was confronted one day by a strange man with a sword in his hand. When asked who he was and what he was there for, the man answered, "I indeed come now as captain of the host of the Lord" (Joshua 5:14). He then informed Joshua that he had already given the city into Joshua's hands and outlined the strategy for taking it. I believe, with most Bible scholars, that this was a preincarnate appearance of Christ; but whether it was or not, it constituted a revelation from God and formed the basis of Joshua's belief that the Lord had delivered Jericho into his hands. Note that the revelation corresponded to the required faith. Joshua had to believe God for a military victory; thus God revealed Himself, not as a shepherd or a guide, but as a Warrior.

The raising of Lazarus provides another example. Arriving in Bethany following the death of Lazarus, Jesus was immediately met by the dead man's sister, Martha, who said, "Lord, if you had been here, my brother would not have died" (John 11:21). When Jesus promised her that Lazarus would rise again, she replied, "I know that he will rise again in the resurrection on the last day'' (John 11:24). Like a good conservative evangelical she believed in the doctrine of the resurrection. But Jesus had something more immediate in mind. He wanted Martha to believe that Lazarus would be raised right then and there. To create that faith He said, ''I am the resurrection and the life'' (John 11:25). The resurrection is more than a doctrine, Jesus was saying; it is a Person—and that Person is here, ready to restore your brother to life. Again, the revelation matched the faith needed.

So then, faith is first and foremost our response to the character of God.

A Revelation of God's Will. Romans 4:17, 18 says, ''(As it is written, 'A FATHER OF MANY NATIONS HAVE I MADE YOU') . . . in hope against hope he believed, in order that he might become a father of many nations, according to that which had been spoken, 'SO SHALL YOUR DESCENDANTS BE.' ''

Observe the sequence. First, God told Abraham that He had made him a father of many nations; then, in response to that revelation, Abraham believed ''in order that he might become'' what God had willed. Abraham's faith was linked to the will of God. And when his faith was united with God's purpose he became in fact what God said he was. It is imperative that we understand that faith operates only within the boundary of God's will. In other words, without a knowledge of God's will there can be no real faith. In prayer, for instance, we cannot ask *in faith* if we are guessing at the will of God. The prayer of faith is the prayer offered in the knowledge of that will; it is not shooting in the dark, hoping we'll get lucky and hit the bullseye. Faith is not man's way of getting his will done in heaven; it is God's way of getting His will done on earth.

Biblical faith, as we saw in chapter three, is a gift from God, and God will not grant us faith to believe something contrary to His will.

Give special attention again to the wording of the text. God said, ''I have made you a father of many nations,'' and Abraham believed in order to become a father of many nations. By faith Abraham cooperated with the purpose of God. And that's the intent of faith: to enable us to cooperate with God. Have you ever noticed how much of our praying is actually an attempt to get God to cooperate with us?

We have this whole thing backwards. We investigate and deliberate, gather a consensus of opinion, call a committee meeting and come up with a plan of what needs to be done and how to do it—then we pray. And often what we're doing is trying to convince God our plan is a good one and to persuade Him to go along with it. We're trying to get God to believe in us, when He wants us to believe in Him; we're trying to get God to cooperate with our plan when He wants us to cooperate with His.

Faith doesn't pull God over to our side; it aligns us with Him and His purpose. God has not said, "If you have enough faith I will do whatever you wish." What He has said is, "If you will put your faith in Me I will enable you to do whatever I want."

MAN'S SIDE — THE HUMAN RESPONSE

Revelation demands a response. God reveals truth, not to satisfy our curiosity or to increase our store of information, but that we might obey. Faith is the positive response to God's revelation. It is man's "Amen" to all that God has declared.

What does this positive response involve? What are we to do? Since Abraham is our model, it is reasonable to assume that the steps taken by him are the ones to be taken by us.

1. Accept the Promise. "In hope against hope he believed" (v. 18). "And being fully assured that what He had promised, He was able also to perform" (v. 21). Hebrews 11:13 describes the faith of Abraham and others like this:

All these died in faith, without receiving the promises, but having seen them, and having welcomed them from a distance, and having confessed that they were strangers and exiles on the earth.

Concerning the promises of God, the writer says that these saints *saw the promises* (that's revelation), and then *welcomed the promises* (that's acceptance). The King James Version says they "embraced" them. The Greek word means "to draw to oneself, to welcome as your own." And that is what we must do with God's promise—draw it to us, take it in our arms and embrace it and say, "This is mine." Though the promise was first made 2,000 years ago, and millions of people have since claimed it, we are to embrace it as though we are the first and only ones to whom God made it.

One of the members of a church I pastored some years ago was a fine tailor. He asked me one Sunday if I had ever owned a tailor-made suit. When I told him I hadn't, he gave the suit I was wearing the once-over and said, "You need one. Come to my shop tomorrow and we'll measure you." A few weeks later I was wearing a beautiful, black, 100 percent mohair tailor-made suit. Do you know what I liked best about that suit? On the inside of the coat, instead of a common brand label, were these words, stitched in red silk thread: "Made exclusively for Ronald Dunn." That's class.

But far more exciting than a tailor-made suit are tailor-made promises! And every promise carries this label: "Made exclusively for Ronald Dunn." That's grace.

Involved in our acceptance of the promise is a commitment to obey. Hebrews 11:8 says, "By faith Abraham, when he was called, obeyed. . . ." His obedience was the evidence of his faith. Believing God always expresses itself in unhesitating obedience. The fourth chapter of John's Gospel relates the incident of a royal official who begged Jesus to come to his house and heal his dying son. Instead of returning with the man to his home, Jesus said, "Go your way; your son lives" (John 4:50). There was the divine revelation: a promise ("Your son lives") and a command ("Go your way"). If the father refused to go back home without Jesus it would indicate unbelief. Belief and obedience are inseparably linked together. The Bible says, "The man believed the word that Jesus spoke to him, and he started off" (John 4:50). Accepting the promise of Jesus, he obeyed.

Because obedience is so vital to faith, a full chapter will be devoted to it later.

One more important point. Romans 4 contains one of the great secrets of faith. Look at the last phrase of verse 16 and the first part of verse 17: ". . . Abraham, who is the father of us all . . . in the sight of Him whom He believed." In the sight of God, Abraham was already the father of many nations. When God looked at Abraham He saw him surrounded by offspring. Why, it would have been easier to count the stars in the sky than to number Abraham's descendants. That's how God saw Abraham. And Abraham accepted God's viewpoint; he saw himself as God saw him.

Seeing things as God sees them is, I believe, the secret of a living, victorious faith. We must see ourselves as God sees us; we must look at life through the eyes of God. And, you know, things look a lot better from up there! From up there the devil looks defeated, my sins are nowhere in sight, every need is supplied, and all problems solved.

2. Renounce All Confidence in Human Resources. Read it again. I didn't say to renounce human resources, only our *confidence* in them. The difference is important, as we will see. But first, look at Romans 4:18: "In hope against hope he believed." The first "hope" refers to Abraham's confidence in God's promise; the second to his confidence in his own ability. His confidence in God was in direct opposition to any confidence in the flesh.

Well, of course. What choice did he have, being a hundred years old? That's just the point. Remember Ishmael? He was Abraham's contribution to God's redemptive program, a product of confidence in his ability to help out God. Perhaps it was to prevent another Ishmael that God waited until Abraham was impotent with age to fulfill the promise. This time there would be no doubt that God alone did it, and God alone would receive the glory. If we are unwilling to renounce human confidence, God may have to renounce it for us. Faith not only trusts God, it distrusts human abilities.

Occasionally I receive a letter from the pastor at a place where I'm to speak. It goes something like this: "We're going to have the greatest meeting in the history of our church, of this town! We have seventy-three committees working around the clock; we've mailed invitations to every residence in the city; your picture is printed on every grocery sack used at the A & P; we've stretched a banner across Main Street; and the day before the meeting starts an airplane is going to drop 100,000 pink leaflets over the city. We can't miss!" But we do. Sometimes God must let us fail rather than allow us to take the credit for something He did.

Don't misunderstand. Faith doesn't renounce the *use* of human resources, only *confidence* in them. Abraham *did* father a son and Sarah *did* give birth to him. There's no record of God delivering Isaac from heaven in a cloud. He used the human apparatus He had created for that very purpose. But while Abraham and Sarah became parents by a very natural and human process, neither of them took credit for what happened. The glory—and the credit—went to God.

I believe we ought to use every available resource—personally, I think the A & P grocery bags is a great idea—but we must never place our confidence in those things. We will never have faith in God's ability until we renounce all faith in our own.

3. *Face the Problem but Focus on the Promise*. Paul continues his description of Abraham's faith in verses 19 and 20: "And without becoming weak in faith he contemplated his own body, now as good as dead since he was about a hundred years old, and the deadness of Sarah's womb; yet, with respect to the promise of God, he did not waver in unbelief, but grew strong in faith, giving glory to God."

Abraham did not shut his eyes to the impossibility of his situation. The Bible says he considered it. Considered is a strong Greek verb indicating a careful consideration resulting in a clear understanding. He didn't just glance at the problem; he looked it squarely in the eye, studying the situation until he fully understood the predicament. And he did it without becoming weak in faith.

You don't have to hide the facts from faith. Faith does not fear contradicting circumstances. To the contrary, true faith becomes stronger when confronted with impossibilities.

But the opposite seems to be true of many modern saints. Our present-day faith is easily intimidated by discouraging facts. Like Gideon we cry, "If the Lord is with us, why then has all this happened to us?" (Judges 6:13). We are outclassed by Abraham, who could calmly consider insurmountable problems "without becoming weak in faith" or "wavering in unbelief."

What was the secret of his faith? Look again at verse 20. "Yet, with respect to the promise of God, he did not waver in unbelief." The key is the phrase, "with respect to the promise of God"; it is emphasized in the Greek text in order to stress that upon which Abraham's faith was focused. The American Standard Version of 1901 reads, "yet, looking unto the promise of God." While examining the problem, Abraham kept his eyes glued to the promise of God. He was so absorbed in the promise, he was not threatened by the problem.

Spurgeon said, "Look at yourself and your doubts will increase. Look at Jesus and they will disappear." Like Peter, if we take our eyes off Jesus we will sink beneath the waves of doubt.

Naturally, we would prefer an unchallenged faith. But faith, like gold that perishes, must be put to the test (1 Peter 1:7). An untried faith is a worthless faith. It is the trial that determines the authenticity of our faith. Face it, your faith will be tested; it will be challenged by critics and contradicted by circumstances. And the only anchor that can hold you in place is the promise of God. Look at the problems—but make your last and longest look at the promise.

Before we leave this point, let me say a word about *doubt*. These verses do not imply that Abraham was totally free of any inward conflict. It is difficult to imagine that not a single doubt passed through his mind. I agree with Calvin, who said,

"The mind is never so enlightened that there are no remains of ignorance, nor the heart so established that there are no misgivings. With these evils of our nature faith maintains a perpetual conflict, in which conflict it is often sorely shaken and put to great stress; but still it conquers." William Sanday, in his classic work on Romans, translates the phrase, "And yet with the promise in view no impulse of unbelief made him hesitate."[2] Certainly there were the "impulses of unbelief"; but with his eyes fixed on the promise, his faith triumphed over all the difficulties.

Don't let doubts make you doubt. With the father of the demon-possessed boy, cry, "Lord, I believe; help thou mine unbelief" (Mark 9:24, KJV).

4. *Rest on God's Faithfulness.* Abraham's act of faith reaches its climax with these words: "He . . . grew strong in faith, giving glory to God, and being fully assured that what He had promised, He was able also to perform" (Romans 4:20, 21). As a result of keeping his eyes on the promise, Abraham grew strong in faith; this strengthening of his faith was expressed by his assurance that God would keep His word, and by giving glory to God.

In other words, Abraham, having accepted God's promise and having acted upon it, left the matter with God, counting on His faithfulness.

Abraham's faith did not weaken when he contemplated the deadness of his body because he knew the condition of his body had nothing whatsoever to do with the outcome. It wasn't Abraham's performance that mattered—it was God's. After all, it was God who made the promise, not Abraham.

Isaac was God's idea. Abraham did not promise God he would produce a son for the purpose of redeeming the world. That was God's promise; therefore, it was God's responsibility.

Again, we have things backwards. We are constantly making promises to God and trying to keep them. And if we promise, then we must perform. And that would make anyone, even Abraham, waver in unbelief. We have not promised God we will supply all our needs—*He* has promised to supply all our needs. We have not promised God we will overcome the world—that's His promise to us. It is God, not man, who has promised to remove the mountains that block our path.

It is this simple: if you make a promise, it's up to you to keep it. If God makes a promise, the responsibility is His. And what God has promised He will perform.

He will perform. Often we try to keep God's promises for Him. What is Ishmael but Abraham's attempt to fulfill God's promise? Faith is believing that what God has promised He can and will do. If God has promised, *He* will perform. Only believe.

Faith, simple faith, the promise sees
And looks to God alone;
Laughs at impossibilities
And cries, "It shall be done."

The issue of such assurance is "giving glory to God." To give glory to God means to openly acknowledge Him as God, ascribing to Him all honor and praise and credit. We glorify God when we believe He will do what He has promised and demonstrate that belief by our actions. Sanday renders the phrase, "He gave praise to God for the miracle that was to be wrought in him."[3] Abraham thanked God in advance for what was to happen. He acted as though the child had already been born.

Faith and praise are inseparable; where you find one you will find the other, supporting and strengthening each other. Faith makes praise shout, and when faith hears the shout of praise it in turn grows stronger and bolder. Praise is the protector of faith, for it is praise that silences the accusing voice of doubt. Learn the art of praise. It is the highest expression of our faith in God.

So there stands our model of faith, Abraham, believing in spite of the facts and giving thanks before the fact. And when we believe as he believed, we will receive as he received.

NOTES

1. William Sanday and A. C. Headlam, *The Epistle to the Romans* (New York: Charles Scribner's Sons, 1901), p. 113.
2. *Ibid.*
3. *Ibid.*

CHAPTER NINE
Does Confession
Bring Possession?

"A single word has sometimes lost or won an empire." When George James wrote those words in *Richelieu* he was nearer biblical truth than he realized. For many Christians, an empire of heavenly blessings has been lost or won because of their words—or lack of them.

While the practice of confession is often abused and misused, there is in the Bible a persistent link between believing and speaking. And while there is more to biblical confession than simply "naming it and claiming it," it is true the inward act of believing must often manifest itself by the outward act of speaking. Confession is faith turned inside out; it is both a sign of the reality of faith and the inevitable product of it.

This bond between faith and confession is emphasized by Jesus in Mark 11:23: "For verily I say unto you, That whosoever shall *say* unto this mountain, Be thou removed, and be thou cast into the sea; and shall not doubt in his heart, but shall believe that those things which he *saith* shall come to pass; he shall have whatsoever he *saith*" (KJV, emphasis added). Notice that Jesus does not say, "He shall have whatsoever he believes," but, "He shall have whatsoever he *says*." Confession and faith are two sides of the same coin, and it is the confession of the mouth that releases the belief of the heart.

This same idea is expressed by Paul in Romans 10:9, 10: "That if you confess with your mouth Jesus as Lord, and believe in your heart that God raised Him from the dead, you shall be saved; for with the heart man believes, resulting in righteousness, and with the mouth he confesses, resulting in salvation." Believing in the heart and confessing with the mouth are both essential with regard to salvation. The belief in the heart must be and inevitably is confessed with the mouth. Commenting on this verse, John Murray says, "Confession without faith would be vain. . . . But likewise faith without confession would be shown to be spurious."[1]

This essential link between confession and faith appears also in Matthew 17:19, 20. Explaining why His disciples were unable to deliver a demon-possessed boy, Jesus said, "Because of the littleness of your faith; for truly I say to you, if you have faith as a mustard seed, you shall say to this mountain, 'Move from here to there,' and it shall move; and nothing shall be impossible to you."

And again in Luke 17:6, Jesus said, "If you had faith like a mustard seed, you would say to this mulberry tree, 'Be uprooted and be planted in the sea'; and it would obey you."

None of these statements can be restricted only to prayer. The words of which Jesus spoke are not words of prayer. When we pray we speak to God; here we are told to speak to a mountain and a tree. I can't remember the last time I prayed to a mountain or a tree—I can't remember a first time. While these promises can be applied to prayer, they are not limited to it. Here Jesus is revealing the phenomenal power of faith when translated into words. And what is even more significant, the act of speaking to a tree or a mountain is not presented as bizarre or extraordinary. On the contrary, *not* to express such belief would be abnormal. As Paul says in 2 Corinthians 4:13 (KJV), "We also believe, and therefore speak." According to Jesus, merely believing in the heart that the mountain will move is sometimes not enough. What is in the heart must be expressed by the mouth. Norman Grubb is right when he calls confession "the summit of faith."[2]

THE PROMINENCE AND POWER OF WORDS

Throughout the Bible, words occupy a place of surprising prominence. God created the world by the power of His spoken word. Hebrews 11:3 tells us that the worlds "were prepared by the word of God." And in Psalm 33:6 we read, "By the word of the Lord the heavens were made, and by the breath of His mouth all their host." Verse 9 says, "For He spoke, and it was done; He commanded, and it stood fast." The unifying thread running through the creation story is, "And God said."

Not only was the world created by the word of God, it is sustained by that same word. Jesus "upholds all things by the word of His power" (Hebrews 1:3). In 2 Peter 3:5, 7 it says "that by the word of God the heavens existed long ago and the earth was formed out of water and by water. . . . But the present heavens and earth by His word are being reserved."

Jesus underscored the awesome importance of words when He said that whoever *speaks a word* against the Holy Spirit shall never be forgiven (Matthew 12:32). It is also worth noting that our Lord always rebuked Satan with spoken words. He cast out demons, not with thoughts, but with words. Paul dealt with the evil spirit that possessed the young slave girl at Philippi, not with thoughts or silent prayer, but by speaking directly to the spirit (Acts 16:18).

One of the most striking examples of the power of words is found in Matthew 12. Addressing the Pharisees, Jesus said, "You brood of vipers, how can you, being evil, speak what is good? For the mouth speaks out of that which fills the heart. The good man out of his good treasure brings forth what is good; and the evil man out of his evil treasure brings forth what is evil. And I say to you, that every careless word that men shall speak, they shall render account for it in the day of judgment. For by your words you shall be justified, and by your words you shall be condemned" (Matthew 12:34–37).

It is "out of that which fills the heart" that men speak. The mouth is like an overflow pipe. It reveals, not merely what is in the heart, but what *fills* the heart, what possesses and dominates the heart. This is why confession is strategic. When we speak we raise the curtain of our heart, exposing its contents. Our confession gives proof of our faith—or our lack of it.

When young David volunteered to fight Goliath, he told Saul, "The Lord who delivered me from the paw of the lion and from the paw of the bear, He will deliver me from the hand of this Philistine" (1 Samuel 17:37). That was a confession of faith. Armed with five smooth stones and his sling, David marched right up to Goliath, looked him straight in the kneecaps, and declared, "This day the Lord will deliver you up into my hands . . . that all the earth may know that there is a God in Israel" (1 Samuel 17:46). While the army of Israel confessed fear and defeat, David confessed victory.

When God instructed Abraham to take Isaac to Moriah and offer him as a sacrifice, Abraham obeyed. The writer of Hebrews reports that Abraham did this by faith, believing that, "God is able to raise men even from the dead; from which he also received him back as a type" (Hebrews 11:19). This faith he expressed by his words; to his servants he said, "Stay here with the donkey, and I and the lad will go yonder; and we will worship and return to you" (Genesis 22:5). To Isaac, who asked about the lamb for the sacrifice, he said, "God will provide for Himself the lamb for the burnt offering" (Genesis 22:8).

Listen to Paul's confession of faith. In chapter three I referred to his never-a-dull-minute excursion to Rome. At the darkest hour, when it looked as if they would all perish in the raging sea, the man of God appeared in the midst of the terrified crowd to tell them he had received assurance from God that all would be saved. Then came the words of confession: "Therefore, keep up your courage, men, for I believe God, that it will turn out exactly as I have been told" (Acts 27:25).

Many more examples are available—Moses at the Red Sea, Gideon before the Midianites, Elijah on Mount Carmel. Always the faith that is in the heart is expressed by the words of the mouth.

Observe the chronology of believing in Hebrews 11:13, 14: "All these died in faith, without receiving the promises, but having seen them, and having welcomed them from a distance, and having confessed that they were strangers and exiles on the earth. For those who say such things make it clear that they are seeking a country of their own.'' These pilgrims of faith

> SAW THE PROMISES,
>   WELCOMED THE PROMISES,
>   CONFESSED THE PROMISES.

God had promised them a city whose Builder and Maker was the Lord. On the basis of that promise they believed that this world was not their home; they were just passing through. By confessing that they were strangers and exiles on the earth they made it clear to those around that they believed God.

WHY CONFESSION?

I am not presuming to lay down any hard and fast rules regarding the exercise of faith, saying you must do it this way. There are no such rules. But I believe there are occasions when the effective exercise of faith will require confession. Here's why.

1. Confession Confirms the Reality of Our Faith. Remember what Jesus said: "The mouth speaks out of that which fills the heart." When the heart is full the mouth will speak. Our confession reveals whether our heart is totally committed and fully believing. One could almost say that there is a sense in which it is not genuine faith until it is confessed. This is certainly true with regard to saving faith.

2. Confession Cements Our Commitment to Trust God. Without a confession of our faith our commitment may be only a halfhearted commitment, one we can easily back out of. And make no mistake about it—we will be tempted to back out of it. Faith will be tested. Circumstances will contradict what God has said. Even our friends may intimidate our faith with

discouraging words and negative attitudes. The light at the end
of the tunnel may turn out to be a train. And if we have kept
our faith hidden in our heart, it will be easier to succumb to
the temptation to cast away our confidence and hedge our bets
with the arm of flesh.

But if that faith has been paraded out of the closet and placed
on the display shelf of confession we will find ourselves agreeing with Ezra. Ezra, you remember, was the man who led the
exiles back to Jerusalem after being released from Babylonian
captivity. Because of the many dangers along the way, he
proclaimed a time of prayer and fasting to seek the Lord for
a safe journey.

His reason for doing this makes interesting reading: ''For I
was ashamed to request from the king troops and horsemen to
protect us from the enemy on the way, because we had said
to the king, 'The hand of our God is favorably disposed to all
those who seek Him, but His power and His anger are against
all those who forsake Him' '' (Ezra 8:22). Ezra's confession
locked him in! Had he not voiced his faith in front of the king
he might have yielded to the temptation to prop it up with the
king's army.

After all, it's easier to trust God when you have an army
backing you up. But you can't go around boasting to the king
about how powerful your God is and then ask for military aid.
Ezra's confession stabilized him and he did not waver in the
hour of testing.

Speaking our faith settles and seals it. Confession is a commitment made, a bridge burned, a flag raised, a vote cast, an
oath taken, a contract signed, an issue decided.

*3. Confession Focuses Our Attention on God and His Prom-
ises.* Confession directs our thoughts away from ourselves and
centers them upon Christ and His faithfulness, preventing us
from becoming introspective. Often after making a commitment of faith we find ourselves traveling through a period of
darkness when our senses fail to register any signs of God's
presence. Doubts arise; our faith becomes fragile. Confession

is a weapon of warfare that enables us to destroy the stronghold of doubt and "every lofty thing raised up against the knowledge of God . . . taking every thought captive to the obedience of Christ" (2 Corinthians 10:5). This is a good way of following Paul's advice in Philippians 4:8, "Finally, brethren, whatever is true, whatever is honorable, whatever is right, whatever is pure, whatever is lovely, whatever is of good repute, if there is any excellence and if anything worthy of praise, let your mind dwell on these things."

4. Confession Encourages Others to Believe. This is the whole point of Hebrews 11. The believers to whom the author writes are going through a severe trial. Their faith is being tested; some are wavering. Encouragement is needed. The author reminds them of others like Abraham and Moses, who endured great trials and who, by faith, emerged victorious. After parading these heroes of faith before their memory, he says, "Therefore, since we have so great a cloud of witnesses surrounding us . . . let us run with endurance the race that is set before us" (Hebrews 12:1). When he speaks of a cloud of witnesses surrounding them, he does not mean that people in heaven are looking down to watch us run. They are not spectators but testifiers. The thought is that the testimonies of Abraham and the others will serve as encouragement, challenging them to believe God and remain steadfast.

There is a beautiful touch in the account of Paul and Silas in the Philippian jail. After beating them, the jailer throws them into the inner prison and binds them with stocks. And then Scripture says, "But about midnight Paul and Silas were praying and singing hymns of praise to God, and the prisoners were listening to them" (Acts 16:25). *And the prisoners were listening to them!* In the midnight trials of our souls, the prisoners are always listening to us. And what they hear will either encourage or discourage them to believe.

5. Confession Glorifies God. Psalm 50:23 tells us that, "Whoso offereth praise glorifieth me" (KJV), and the confession of faith is one of the highest forms of praise. The word "confess" means to *say the same thing*, and in confession we are simply saying the same thing God has said, affirming our faith in His Word. What could please God more than hearing his children boldly voice their faith in their heavenly Father?

When my son was about ten years old, I chauffeured him and one of his friends to a party at the church. They were riding in the back seat, having, of all things, a big theological discussion. Turning down the radio so I could eavesdrop on this phenomenon, I overheard my son drive home a point by repeating almost word for word something I had said in a sermon the Sunday before. I was surprised and delighted— surprised that he had listened carefully enough to remember the phrase so accurately; and delighted that he had adopted it as his own conviction. It was a special joy to hear my words coming from the mouth of my son. Surely God must experience a similar joy when He hears His words coming back to Him from the lips of His believing children.

CAUTIONS CONCERNING CONFESSION

I have observed among many Christians a tendency to turn the principle of confession into something magical or psychical. Like many biblical truths, confession may be driven to the point of excess and become totally unbiblical. Misunderstood and misused confession may become a yoke of bondage. Let me mention three ways in which this can happen.

1. A Magic Formula. One night after an exhausting preaching service I climbed into the car of a friend and collapsed in the back seat. "Man, I am bushed," I groaned. Instantly my friend whirled around, pointed his finger at me, and said, "Don't say that! That's a negative confession." I thought it a rather honest confession; I *was* bushed. Frankly, I've been around some well-meaning souls who have so twisted this idea that, had they been present at the crucifixion, I'm convinced that when Jesus cried out, "I thirst," they would have rebuked Him for making a negative confession.

A "bad" or "negative" confession is confessing something contrary to what God has said, and God has not said that we would be immune to physical exhaustion. Even Jesus grew weary and needed rest and refreshment.

The wife of a preacher I know was invited to a covered-dish luncheon at a neighboring church. When she walked in with her culinary contribution, one of the ladies asked what she had brought.

"Deviled eggs," she said.

Immediately the woman flung out her hands and said, "I bind that in the name of Jesus!"

Unperturbed, the preacher's wife said, "You can bind it all you want, it's still deviled eggs."

While our words are important, they are not magic. Merely confessing something doesn't make it so. Remember, confession doesn't create faith; faith creates confession.

Prevalent today is the "name it and claim it" syndrome—the idea that you will have whatever you say (literally), even if you don't mean what you say. A casually spoken word, even, can result in either a curse or a blessing, depending on what you said. If you confess good things, good things will happen to you; if you confess bad things, bad things will happen to you. You have whatever you say.

The "name it and claim it" folk believe that if you confess wealth, you will be wealthy; if you confess health, you will be healthy. Some go so far as to say that if you casually say, "I'm afraid I'll have cancer someday," you at that moment give the devil authority, which before he did not have, to give you cancer. Saying something negative, according to this view, actually puts you under a curse of words and gives Satan the right to do whatever you have said. You must, therefore, be careful at all times of what you say.

To live under such a bondage is both unhealthy and unscriptural. Only as our confession reflects the revealed will of God does it have validity. Such power is vested, not in *our* words but in the Word of God, confessed and obeyed.

And then there have been some fever-ridden folk who, between their sneezes and coughs, kept saying, "I'm healed,

I'm healed.'' When I questioned the fever and the sneezing and the coughing, I was told these things were just symptoms. They were healed, they explained, but the symptoms remained, and unless they held fast their confession of healing, the illness would return. I have no desire to make light of such sincerity, but I fail to see the value of a healing that leaves you suffering with the symptoms. It was not that way in the biblical healings. All the healings in the Bible were complete—the symptoms never stayed around once the disease left. I believe this is a case of assigning to the mere act of confession a power that God has not given it and that it borders on superstition.

2. *Priming the Pump*. Teachers of faith often tell us that when we are believing God for something specific we should confess it to someone else. If I am trusting God for one hundred dollars I ought to tell someone what I am believing God for. And there are instances in which this should be done. But our confession may become a subtle way of priming the pump. I may find myself choosing to make my confession to a wealthy friend, hoping he will ''feel led'' to supply the money. That would encourage my faith more than making my confession to a beggar. As someone has said, ''We have not because we hint not.''

I pastored a large and very generous church and I'm certain that if I confessed to the members one Sunday morning that I was believing God for a new suit, I would have had it before the day was out. I'm not saying that is wrong, but for me to use that as an example of faith and of the power of confession would be wrong, because not everyone has a large congregation eager to satisfy his needs. We preachers have an advantage that others do not have and we must be careful about making our particular experience the standard for others.

A good rule of confession is this: Make your confession to someone who cannot fulfill your request.

3. *Positive Thinking*. The line between psychic power and spiritual power is almost imperceptible and the two are easily

confused. Psychic power is often mistaken for spiritual power. We're all familiar with the story of the fellow who arrives at the office feeling great, but after a few scheming friends tell him he looks bad, he goes home sick. The concentration of the mind does often determine the direction of the life; and faith has sometimes been defined as psychic power channeled in good and godly directions. But that is not biblical faith. The confession of faith is not a mind-over-matter proposition.

This is, I think, the mistake often made about positive thinking. Again I want to emphasize that I am not criticizing positive thinking as such. Everyone ought to possess a positive mental attitude; I hate to be around someone with a negative mental attitude. But again, positive thinking is not biblical faith.

Positive thinking says, "Believe and it will be so."

Biblical faith says, "Believe because God has said it is so."

Positive thinking is based on our own desires—if we believe hard enough we will get what we want. Faith is based upon God's desire for us as revealed in His word.

Positive thinking is in the end merely believing in yourself. Biblical faith is repudiating all confidence in the flesh and believing in the Lord.

Norman Grubb offers this word of caution concerning confession:

The word of faith, if a mere word, can be a shallow sham. Faith is the whole man in action, *and the word of faith includes the heart and mind that is in tune with the will of God and His written revelation, the voice that speaks the word of faith, and all subsequent action that is in full conformity with the position of faith which has been declared.*[3]

WHAT, THEN, ARE WE TO CONFESS?

We are to confess three things: we are to confess that

WE ARE WHAT GOD SAYS WE ARE . . .
     WE HAVE WHAT GOD SAYS WE HAVE . . .
          WE CAN DO WHAT GOD SAYS WE CAN DO.

Remember: confession is agreeing with God, saying the same thing He has said. That which we confess must be that which God has already spoken to us. This eliminates the idea that if I want something, all I need do is confess it and I will have whatever I say. As already noted, confession does not create faith; faith creates confession. The idea originates with God, not with us.

Biblical faith is imparted to us by God through His word— the external Word of the Bible and the internal word of the Spirit. We must *first* have a word from God. And it is this point that many miss. In their fervent rush to use the newly discovered key of faith they forget that it unlocks only those doors God has made—not the doors created by our wishes.

But don't despair. There are riches enough behind God's doors of grace to satisfy the longing of every heart. He still opens His hand to satisfy the desire of every creature. And once we begin to explore the treasures those doors conceal we will thank God for not abandoning us to the fool's gold of our own capricious desires.

NOTES

1. John Murray, *The Epistle to the Romans, Volume II* (Grand Rapids: Wm. B. Eerdmans Publishing Co., 1965), p. 56.
2. Norman Grubb, *The Law of Faith* (Ft. Washington: Christian Literature Crusade, 1947), p. 112. Taken from copyrighted material used by permission of the Christian Literature Crusade, Fort Washington, PA 19034.
3. *Ibid.*, p. 116.

CHAPTER TEN
How to Complete Your Faith

The goal of faith is to turn the things promised into the things possessed. And once we realize the immeasurable wealth contained in God's promises, no sacrifice will be too great, no discipline too severe, for faith to reach its goal. This is the pearl of great price and we will be willing to sell all else in order to possess it. But, unfortunately, the faith of many Christians never reaches its goal. Like exhausted runners, they find their faith collapses just short of the finish line. More than a few once-eager souls have said to me, "Well, I tried faith, but it didn't work for me."

But the problem is many of these discouraged believers did not *complete* their faith. For faith to reach its goal, it must be completed. What do I mean by "completing your faith"? The epistle of James uses this phrase in describing the faith of Abraham.

Was not Abraham our father justified by works, when he offered up Isaac his son on the altar? You see that faith was working with his works, and as a result of the works, faith was perfected [completed, marginal reading]; and the Scripture was fulfilled which says, "AND ABRAHAM BELIEVED GOD,

AND IT WAS RECKONED TO HIM AS RIGHTEOUSNESS,'' and he was called the friend of God (James 2:21–23).

Let's take a closer look at the phrase ''faith was perfected.'' The word translated *perfect* means ''to bring to an end, to accomplish, to bring to maturity, to fulfill its purpose.'' Charles B. Williams in his translation renders the phrase, ''faith was made complete.'' The Beck translation is especially vivid: ''. . . reached its goal.''

Perfected faith is faith that has reached its goal, faith that has accomplished its purpose. It has completed the task assigned it. Abraham's goal was to be righteous before God. The task assigned to his faith was to obtain righteousness—and it completed its task.

But how? What did Abraham do to perfect his faith? James gives the answer in these words: ''Was not Abraham our father justified by works, when he offered up Isaac his son on the altar? You see that faith was working with his works, *and as a result of the works, faith was perfected*'' (vv. 21, 22, emphasis added).

Faith is perfected, or completed, by works. Abraham's experience is Exhibit A in James' argument concerning faith and works. This argument, beginning with verse 14 of chapter two, describes two men who claim to have faith. But only one claim is legitimate. One man has faith (so he says) and the other has faith plus something else—works. James asserts that the latter is the genuine article.

The faith versus works issue is a controversy familiar to all students of the New Testament. Some argue that when James says we are justified by works as well as by faith, he is contradicting Paul, who teaches that we are justified by faith alone (Romans 3:28). Paul plainly states that Abraham was justified by faith without works.

But no real conflict exists between Paul and James. While both use the same word, they attach different meanings to it. For instance, when Paul speaks of ''work'' he is referring to the keeping of the Jewish ceremonial law. But James has in mind the everyday good works of the Christian, which, according to the apostle, are the product and proof of salvation. Again, when Paul talks of being justified, he means our righteous standing before God, our having been declared righteous by God.

But James uses the term in the sense of vindication, being *seen to be righteous* by those who observe our behavior. In other words, Paul is referring to our justification before God, and James to our justification before men. God sees our faith and because of it declares us to be righteous. But men can see our faith only when it is recast in the form of good works.

James says, "But someone may well say, 'You have faith, and I have works; show me your faith without the works, and I will show you my faith by my works'" (James 2:18). Genuine faith always identifies itself by works. If there are no works, there is no faith. Faith without works is but a hollow profession, and works without faith nothing but sterile activity. What breath is to the body, works are to faith. If, James says, a man claims to have faith but there is no visible evidence, no good works issuing from his life, his claim is false.

The Bible is uncompromisingly clear on this point. Faith without works is dead, able to accomplish nothing. If it is to reach its goal, faith must work. These verses suggest two kinds of works necessary to complete our faith.

COOPERATING WORKS

"You see that faith co-operated with his good deeds, and by his good deeds faith was made complete" (James 2:22, Williams Translation).

Faith expresses itself in works. Faith and works have often been seen as antagonists, two opposing qualities between which we must choose. Those who choose works often accuse the faith-folk of laziness and indifference. Those who side with faith sometimes accuse the work-folk of laboring in the energy of the flesh. But the two are not mutually exclusive. They are part and parcel of each other, and to separate one from the other destroys them both. J. B. Phillips gives a good description of this in his translation: "Can't you see that his faith and his actions were, so to speak, *partners* . . .?" (emphasis added). I like to think of the relationship between faith and works as "Faith and Son, Incorporated"—and the son's name is Works.

True faith is active. Read again the account of the faith of the Old Testament saints in Hebrews 11. The writer describes their faith by talking about their works. They *did something*. Believing God does not mean lounging lazily about with our arms folded and "letting God do it." Faith is acting on the revealed will of God.

To believe God is to obey God. In Hebrews 3:18, 19, the writer, speaking of Israel's failure to enter the Promised Land, says, "And to whom did He swear that they should not enter His rest, but to those who were disobedient? And so we see that they were not able to enter because of unbelief." In verse 18 he says they could not enter because of disobedience; in verse 19 the reason given is unbelief.

Well, which was it—disobedience or unbelief? It was both. Disobedience and unbelief are two sides of the same coin. Disobedience *is* unbelief. Regardless of how loudly we may claim to believe the Bible, we believe only as much of it as we obey.

When was Abraham justified? At what precise point was his faith completed and credited to his account as righteousness? "Was not Abraham our father justified by works, *when he offered up Isaac his son on the altar*? (James 2:21, emphasis added). Abraham's faith reached its goal when he did exactly as God had commanded.

One of our major problems is *reversed responsibilities*. By this I mean that we often try to get God to do our part while we attempt to do His. For example, take a common approach to evangelism. Many Christians, especially preachers, feel it is their responsibility to produce evangelistic results, and they measure their success by how many people they win to Christ. Don't get me wrong—I believe witnessing for Christ and winning others to saving faith in Him is the responsibility of every believer. I'm convinced one of the greatest sins of the modern church is its failure to share the gospel of Christ on a one-to-one basis.

But sometimes in our eagerness to have converts we stoop to Madison Ave. gimmicks and psychological tricks, or we weaken the demands of the gospel to make it easy for reluctant repentants. And as a result, many of the converts listed on church rolls are there, not by the power of God, but through the persuasive cleverness of man. As Paul puts it, their faith stands in the wisdom of man rather than in the power of God (1 Corinthians 2:5).

Such an approach trespasses on God's responsibility. It is God who causes the growth (1 Corinthians 3:6, 7). Man can plow, plant, and water, but only God can give the increase.

But man has a responsibility. He must plant and water. God has promised to give the increase, but we must cooperate with Him by planting and watering. God will not plant and water—that is our responsibility. But, regrettably, many of us leave to God that which is our clear duty.

Let's imagine that we are driving through a rural area and we stop at a farmhouse. Sitting on the front porch, rocking slowly back and forth in an ancient rocker, is the farmer.

"What are you doing?" we ask.

"Farming," he says.

"What are you raising?"

"Corn."

But as we look out over his fields we see nothing but unplowed and unplanted ground. "Excuse us, sir," we say, "but you haven't plowed your fields. And it doesn't look like you've planted any corn."

"Yep, that's right."

"We don't understand."

"I'm farming by faith. Believing God for a crop."

"But," we protest, "shouldn't you be *doing* something—maybe planting some corn?"

"I *am* doing something," he says.

"What?"

"I'm praying. Praying and believing. Praise the Lord!"

If every farmer exercised that kind of faith we would all have starved to death long ago. But that is no more ridiculous than some of the ideas about faith floating around. There is something we must do. Abiding in the Lord is not *idling* in the Lord. Faith must express itself by working.

Faith encourages us to work. The farmer doesn't plow his fields and plant his crops because he *hopes* something will come of it; he plows and plants because he *knows* something will come of his labor. Nor do we go out to the field of service to toil and labor, *hoping* something will happen. We work because we *know* something will happen. Just as the farmer has faith in the laws of sowing and reaping, we have faith in the promises of God.

A Christian shares the gospel with others because he has faith in the Word of God and in the operation of the Holy Spirit and knows that his labor in the Lord is not in vain. Going back to Paul's words in 1 Corinthians 3:6, 7: one man plants, another waters, but God gives the increase. And that is what encourages us to plant and water. Faith says, "God *will* cause the growth. Regardless of how barren things may appear, God is faithful and will bless the planting and the watering." Faith encourages us to do our part and trust God to do His.

CORRESPONDING WORKS

"Now what use is it, my brothers, for a man to say he 'has faith' if his actions do not *correspond* with it?" (James 2:14, Phillips Translation, emphasis added). To illustrate his point, James tells of a brother who is naked and destitute of food. Seeing his need, we speak a word of faith, "Go in peace, be warmed and filled." And that is all we do. Now James says that kind of faith is dead. Unless we do something practical about the situation, our so-called faith is a mockery.

OK, so we must do something practical to show our faith. What shall we do? Paint the church? Sing a hymn? Preach a sermon on world hunger? None of these things would alleviate the man's suffering. It is not enough to do something; we must do something that corresponds to his need. In other words, James says, we ought to give him the things he needs; give him some food and clothing. That is corresponding works.

If a farmer really believes in the laws of sowing and reaping, he doesn't say, "I'll go to Africa as a missionary and that will cultivate my fields." If he believes in sowing and reaping, he will sow and reap.

For every act of faith there is a corresponding work. For example, Hebrews 11:9 tells us that Abraham believed that God would raise Isaac from the dead. Now what was the corresponding work that cooperated with his faith? To sacrifice Isaac as God commanded.

Rahab the harlot believed God would enable Israel to conquer Jericho. What was her corresponding work that cooperated with her faith? She hid the two spies from the king's men and helped them escape from the city. She switched rather than fought.

God told Joshua He would part the flooding waters of the Jordan River so all Israel could cross on dry ground. But the Jordan was sort of like one of those electric-eye doors at the supermarket—you must step toward it before it will open. Scripture says that "when those who carried the ark came into the Jordan, and the feet of the priests carrying the ark were dipped in the edge of the water . . . that the waters which were flowing down from above stood and rose up in one heap . . . while all Israel crossed on dry ground" (Joshua 3:15–17). The waters parted (faith reached its goal) when the priests, in obedience to God's command, stepped into the water. That was the corresponding work that cooperated with their faith.

The application to present-day faith is inescapable. Are you facing a Jordan River that stubbornly refuses to part, in spite of all your praying and believing? *Check your obedience.* Is it up-to-date? As far as you know, have you done all God has instructed you to do? Or are you waiting for the waters to part first before you put your foot to the edge?

This principle of cooperating and corresponding works is

found in Jesus' healing of the ten lepers recorded in Luke 17. The lepers, seeing Jesus enter their village, cried out, "Jesus, Master, have mercy on us!" (v. 13). Luke tells us that when Jesus saw them, "He said to them, 'Go and show yourselves to the priests.' " That was significant. When a leper was healed the law required that he be "certified"—cured by the priests, before he was allowed once again to take his place as a normal citizen.

But these lepers were not healed; they were still afflicted with that loathsome disease when Jesus commanded them to go to the priests. How could they act as though they were healed when they weren't? It isn't hard to imagine the thoughts that might have raced through their minds—the priests would rebuke them, the people would mock them. They would be the laughingstock of the whole village. Being a leper was bad enough without that.

But the Bible says, "And it came about that as they were going, they were cleansed" (Luke 17:14). When were they cleansed? *As they were going.* As they were obeying. They stepped toward the door and it opened; they placed their feet in the water and the river parted. Their faith was completed by their cooperating and corresponding work. Had they insisted on waiting until they were healed before going to the priests, they would have died lepers.

One week in February of 1971, I was preparing a sermon on 2 Timothy 2:4: "No soldier in active service entangles himself in the affairs of everyday life, so that he may please the one who enlisted him as a soldier." The Lord spoke to me about my own entanglement. I was in financial bondage and had been for as long as I could remember. If God had wanted to move me to another field of service it would have taken extradition papers to get me out of Texas.

I was still making monthly payments on things I had bought for Christmas in 1969. We lived on the crumbling brink of financial disaster. I tried to save money, but every time our savings account got up to three or four dollars we had to take it out for some emergency. From my own experience and from the marriage counseling I had done as a minister, I knew that most of the problems between husbands and wives could be traced back to money problems.

On edge, irritable, quick-tempered, I found it impossible to give myself wholly to being a husband or father or minister with the strain of indebtedness that constantly harassed me. If God could deliver me from this, it would be a miracle second only to creation.

Believing that God wanted to and was able to liberate me from this entanglement, I knelt in my study and claimed His deliverance and, to cement the decision, announced my commitment to my wife and to my secretary. I believed God and publicly confessed my faith.

Guess what happened? Nothing. Things didn't improve one bit, financially. But my mind was at rest; I knew God had spoken to my heart and I was simply waiting for His promise to be fulfilled. But as time dragged by, I began to wonder—and worry.

Then, in May of 1972, God spoke to me through another verse: Luke 6:38, which says, "Give, and it will be given to you; good measure, pressed down, shaken together, running over, they will pour into your lap. For whatever measure you deal out to others, it will be dealt to you in return." The verse wasn't new to me. I had read it many times, even preached on it. I believed it; it was in the Bible so I had to. But it had never come alive to my heart, had never been made real to me as it was that day. I knew that *that* was how God intended to deliver me from financial bondage. Here was a work that cooperated and corresponded to my faith.

Now, concerning that verse: I couldn't escape its meaning. I had been saying that when I got straightened out financially I was going to be more liberal in my giving. As a matter of fact, that was one of the reasons I was anxious to get out of debt—I wanted to be able to give freely and generously to the cause of Christ and to the needs of others. But I was practically eligible for foreign aid myself. So I told myself that when I got it I would give it. And then I met up with this verse.

Instead of saying, "When you get it, give it," it had the audacity to say, *"When you give it, you will get it."*

I said, "Lord, I can't afford to give."

He said, "You can't afford not to."

But what if my interpretation of that verse was wrong? I had never been as fastidious about correct interpretation as I was at that moment. Someone once asked me why I use so many illustrations involving money, and I replied that if people can learn to trust God in matters of finance, they can learn to trust Him about anything. In the battle of faith, money is usually the last stronghold to fall.

I decided to give it a try. I was willing to obey the light I had and trust God either to confirm or refute my interpretation of Luke 6:38. A few days later I was asked to conduct the funeral of a woman who was not a member of our church. Afterward a member of the family handed me an envelope containing a fifty dollar bill. It was the first time in my ministry I had ever been paid for conducting a funeral. I stuck the bill in my pocket.

That night after our midweek prayer service, as I walked from the worship center to my office, I ran into a missionary on furlough who had visited our services that evening. As I talked with him, the Lord seemed to say, "Give him the fifty dollars in your back pocket." I excused myself and hurried into my office, wondering where in the world that voice had come from and how it knew exactly where I was keeping that fifty dollar bill. "That could be the devil," I said.

I thought about it a while, then said, "Lord, if this is really You speaking—if you really want me to give this fifty dollars to that missionary, let me know beyond any doubt." When it comes to parting with fifty dollars, you can't be too careful.

A few minutes later I left my office. If the missionary was gone (and he should have been since it was so late), I would have known that it had not been the Lord speaking to me. But when I walked outside, there he was, standing right where I had left him thirty minutes before. He was standing there by himself, as though he were waiting for someone—or something. I fished the fifty from my back pocket, gave it a last loving look, went over to the missionary, and pressed it into his hand. ''The Lord told me to give this to you,'' I said.

And that was the beginning of my exodus from the land of bondage. By October of that year I was out of debt. Since then I have been able to meet every financial obligation on time, with enough left over to give generously to every good cause God has laid on my heart. God did not give me a thousand barrels of oil to salt away in a bank vault; He gave me one barrel of oil that never runs dry. I believe the best description of financial freedom is found in 2 Corinthians 9:8: ''And God is able to make all grace abound to you, that always having all sufficiency in everything, you may have an abundance for every good deed.''

God's promise to me was threefold: (1) every need adequately supplied; (2) every financial obligation met on time; (3) able to give generously to every good cause. But the promise did not become a possession until my works corresponded and cooperated with my faith.

FOR INSTANCE . . .

Few verses are as precious to believers as Romans 8:28: ''And we know that God causes all things to work together for good to those who love God, to those who are called according to His purpose.'' That's a fantastic promise. Just think of it— God takes everything that comes our way, good and bad, and by His sovereign power works it all together for our good and His glory. Whatever happens, God is going to see to it that it works out for our good. Ask the average Christian if he believes that verse and he will answer with a hearty ''Amen!''

Do you believe that verse? I do. Then why do we grumble and gripe so much? Why do we hit the panic button when something unexpected happens that foils our well-laid plans? That is hardly a corresponding reaction. The corresponding work that cooperates with our faith is to stop complaining and "in everything give thanks; for this is God's will for you in Christ Jesus" (1 Thessalonians 5:18).

A NEW GOLDEN RULE

Consider the prayer promise in Matthew 7:11. Jesus said, "If you then, being evil, know how to give good gifts to your children, how much more shall your Father who is in heaven give what is good to those who ask Him!" What is the act that corresponds to faith in this case? Prayer, of course, is the obvious answer. But, I think, the incorrect one.

Let's look at the following verse. It begins with the word "therefore," which means Jesus is about to make a practical application of a truth just stated. "Therefore whatever you want others to do for you, do so for them. . . ." We call this the Golden Rule; but I'm afraid many people read it the wrong way. Like this: "Therefore whatever you *don't* want others to do to you, *don't* do to them."

In other words, if I don't want someone to punch me in the nose, I ought not to punch anybody else in the nose. And if I haven't done anything to anyone today that I wouldn't want done to me, I think I have obeyed the Golden Rule. But that is not what Jesus said or meant. The Golden Rule is positive, not negative. We are to take the initiative and *do* for others what we would want done for us.

Now see the connection between verse 11 and verse 12. In prayer we are asking God to do good things for us. All right; if we want God to do good things for us we must do good things for others. In short, we must treat others the way we want God to treat us. You see, the Golden Rule is actually this: *Do unto others as you would have God do unto you.*

Prayer is an act of faith, and the corresponding work that cooperates with that faith is doing good to others. If I want God to give me good things I must give good things to others. And if I really believe that God is going to give me good things, I can easily afford to give good things to others. I am convinced that many unanswered prayers can be traced back to our failure to obey this command.

WISDOM — OURS FOR THE ASKING

James 1:5 is a promise that has meant much to me in recent years. The apostle says, "But if any of you lacks wisdom, let him ask of God, who gives to all men generously and without reproach, and it will be given to him." This promise is made within the context of trials in the believer's life. James tells us that if we do not know what to do during a time of testing, we can ask God for wisdom and He will provide all that we need.

For years I approached that promise like this: In the midst of a trying situation I would ask God for wisdom, claiming this particular promise. Then I would wait for God to pump some wisdom into my brain. I would wait and wait but rarely feel any wiser. I saw no fiery writing in the sky instructing me what to do; there was no sudden surge of divine insight gushing into my mind. Then I would pray again, hoping that this time my aim would be good enough to hit the bullseye. Still no wisdom; still no flutter of wings as angels bent low to whisper the secret wisdom of heaven in my ear.

Then came a period when my wife and I lived in a constant whirlwind of trials, with every day demanding wise and critical decisions. I felt anything but wise; I was overwhelmed by the relentless pressure created by the situation. Desperation drove me again to this verse, and God in His goodness opened my eyes to its truth. Studying the verse afresh, I zeroed in on the last phrase: "and it will be given him." Period. Just like that.

In the following verse James says that we are to ask in faith "without any doubting." *Doubting* translates a Greek word that means to be at odds with oneself, wavering between two opinions, separating one from the other. It expresses a hesitation to act affirmatively—a perfect description of what I had been doing. Even as I prayed, I kept separating things I thought possible from the things I thought impossible.

After praying I was hesitant to act, unsure of myself, uncertain if God had heard me. Categorizing things as possible or impossible is rank unbelief, for with God there is only one category: possible. My hesitation to act after asking God for wisdom was unbelief that voided my prayer.

I concluded that, to receive the answer, I must act on the assumption that God had given me the asked-for wisdom. He had promised to give it and I had the right to assume that *what seemed to be the wise decision was the right decision*, the decision that God Himself would make. In exercising my wisdom, I was exercising His wisdom. And so I did that which cooperated with and corresponded to my prayer of faith.

I made the decision as best I knew how, believing God was imparting to me His wisdom and insight. How could I claim God was giving me wisdom if I was afraid to make a decision? And I am happy to report that time has proven that every decision I made during those critical days was the correct one.

I cannot emphasize too strongly the importance of this principle. For every affirmation of faith there is a cooperating and corresponding act of obedience. The goal of faith is to get us out of the foyer and into every room of God's abundance. But that goal can be achieved only as we bring our obedience up-to-date by acting upon the Word of God.

CHAPTER ELEVEN
Waiting for the Promise

"Bible promises," said Spurgeon, "are like checks drawn on heaven's bank that we endorse by faith and present to God for payment."

True. But sometimes the checks are post-dated! One of the most disturbing discoveries we make in the life of faith is that God does not operate according to our time schedule. We assume God will respond immediately to our prayers, and we rise from our knees expecting to find the answer standing before us. But more often than not, there is a waiting period between the asking and the receiving. And to twentieth-century Christians, this is a big problem.

In these days of instant coffee and instant credit, we have a low tolerance for delay. We demand everything right now, if not sooner. Eric Hoffer writes:

If one were to pick the chief trait which characterizes the temper of our time it would be impatience. Tomorrow has become a dirty word.[1]

The interim between asking and receiving is a precarious time for the believer. His faith, growing more frustrated and fragile with each unfulfilled day, becomes vulnerable to the attacks of the enemy. Satan, ever the opportunist, would have us think that God's delay is God's denial; he whispers in our ear, "Hath God said?" Our faith droops, our feelings sell out to the enemy, and doubt unpacks its suitcase for an extended visit.

Let's face it: if we are going to know the life of faith we must learn how to handle what J. Sidlow Baxter calls "those strange delays."[2]

BETTER LATE THAN EVER

The delays are as much a part of God's purpose as are the fulfillments. In fact, *the delays will usually prove a greater blessing than the fulfillments*. The full story as to why God delays His answers is buried in the mystery of His infinite wisdom; but here are some clues.

1. Sometimes God waits until we are spiritually mature enough to handle the blessing we are seeking. Every parent knows that he must determine not only what is good for his child, but also *when* it is good for him. The right thing given at the wrong time can be a curse rather than a blessing.

2. God may test the sincerity of our desire by withholding the object of our request. He is a rewarder of those who diligently seek Him (Hebrews 11:6).

3. God uses delay to strengthen our character. Remember that the "testing of your faith produces endurance. And let endurance have its perfect result, that you may be perfect and complete, lacking in nothing" (James 1:3, 4). God may use delay to draw us into a deeper communion with Him, the delay causing us to seek Him more earnestly.

4. Sometimes God withholds the blessing until the blessing becomes of secondary importance. It is dangerously easy to fix our heart on the blessing rather than the Blesser, on the gift instead of the Giver. Only when the Blesser overshadows the blessing are we truly ready to receive it. Hebrews 11:6 tells us that God is a rewarder of those who seek *Him*, not the reward. To repeat the words of Charles Wesley,

Thy gifts alone cannot suffice,
Except Thyself be given,
For Thy presence makes my paradise,
And where Thou art is heaven.

There is an intriguing statement concerning Abraham's faith in Hebrews 11. The writer says, "By faith he lived as an alien in the land of promise, as in a foreign land, dwelling in tents with Isaac and Jacob, fellow-heirs of the same promise; for he was looking for the city which has foundations, whose architect and builder is God" (Hebrews 11:9, 10). And then the writer sums up the faith of Abraham and the others with these words: "But as it is, they desire a better country, that is a heavenly one" (Hebrews 11:16).

Abraham lived *as an alien in the land of promise . . . looking for the city whose builder was God.* God promised to lead Abraham to a land of his own, and He did. Yet when Abraham arrived in that land, when at last he received the fulfillment of God's promise, he was not satisfied. Although he was in the land of promise, he looked beyond that land to the literal presence of God. To Abraham there was something more to be desired than the promise of God—the presence of God. Perhaps when he began the journey the land meant everything; but by the time he had reached his destination, God had become everything.

God's blessings are not an end in themselves. They are the means God uses to draw us to Himself. "The goodness of God leadeth thee to repentance." God may have to withhold the blessing until we come to love Him for Himself instead of what He can do for us; or, as someone put it, until we seek His face instead of His hand. God honors the faith that desires His fellowship more than His favors.

With God, *timing* is more important than time, and whatever the reason for the delay, we may rest assured that His timing is always perfect and that the delay is a vital part of His redemptive purpose. Let us learn to pray with George Matheson: "My Father, help me to learn that I am heir to possessions which exceed my present holding! They exceed my present *power* to hold—they are waiting for my summer. Do I ever thank Thee for the blessings which Thou postponest? I am afraid not. I am like the prodigal: I want to get *all at once* the portion that falleth to me; and, where it is not given, I deem it is refused. Teach me, O Lord, the beauty of Thy delayed answers.''[3]

HANGING-ON FAITH

Faith can be seen as existing on two levels: faith as an initial act; and faith as a continuing activity or attitude. There is the faith that brings us to Jesus with our need; and there is the faith that keeps us there when the need is not immediately supplied. C. S. Lewis said, "Faith is the art of holding on to things your reason once accepted, in spite of changing moods.''[4]

Of the various dimensions of faith, this is the most vital; and it is this kind of faith, more than any other, that we will be called upon to exercise. When everything we once easily believed seems suddenly improbable and illogical, it is "hanging-on" faith that holds us on course and keeps our eyes fixed on the unfailing promises of God.

Jesus says to us, as He said to Jairus, "Now don't be afraid, go on believing" (Luke 8:50, Phillips). Having presented the promise to God and having claimed it as ours, we must "strike the pose of faith" and hold it until, in God's time, the promise is fulfilled.

Easier said than done. How do I strike this pose of faith and hold it against the onslaught of doubt and discouragement? Hebrews 10 contains a powerful example of "hanging-on" faith. From the passage that follows we can learn the secret of waiting.

But remember the former days, when, after being enlightened, you endured a great conflict of sufferings, partly, by being made a public spectacle through reproaches and tribulations, and partly by becoming sharers with those who were so treated.

For you showed sympathy to the prisoners, and accepted joyfully the seizure of your property, knowing that you have for yourselves a better possession and an abiding one. Therefore, do not throw away your confidence, which has a great reward. For you have need of endurance, so that when you have done the will of God, you may receive what was promised.

> *FOR YET IN A VERY LITTLE WHILE,*
> *HE WHO IS COMING WILL COME, AND WILL*
> *NOT DELAY.*
> *BUT MY RIGHTEOUS ONE SHALL LIVE BY FAITH:*
> *AND IF HE SHRINKS BACK, MY SOUL HAS NO*
> *PLEASURE IN HIM.*

But we are not of those who shrink back to destruction, but of those who have faith to the preserving of the soul (Hebrews 10:32–39).

The Christians to whom the author wrote were facing persecution so severe that their faith was threatened with collapse. There was even talk of defecting. To shore up the walls of their sagging faith and to enable them to emerge victorious from this trial, he reminded them of their previous trials and how they overcame them. He speaks of a "great reward" (v. 35) and of receiving "what was promised" (v. 36). The whole passage dovetails into that last phrase in verse 36—that is the end toward which everything moves: that "you may receive what was promised." Quite simply, the writer is telling them what they must do to receive what was promised.

This hanging-on faith that knows how to wait for the promise revolves around three key words: *confidence, obedience,* and *endurance.*

WAITING FOR THE PROMISE REQUIRES CONFIDENCE BASED ON GOD'S PAST FAITHFULNESS.

In verse 35 the author says, "Therefore, do not throw away your confidence, which has a great reward." Confidence, often translated "boldness," is one of the great words of the New Testament and is a chief characteristic of believers. It means conspicuous courage in the face of adversity. It is the ability to face trials with a courageous calmness, to respond with Christlike meekness when wronged.

It is Job saying, "Though He slay me yet will I serve Him." It is Paul and Silas in prison with bleeding backs, yet singing praises at midnight. It is Peter and the apostles, when threatened by the religious leaders, saying, "We must obey God rather than men." It is Jesus, being reviled, refusing to revile in return, who, as Peter says, "While suffering . . . uttered no threats, but kept entrusting Himself to Him who judges righteously" (1 Peter 2:23).

The word "therefore" points back to the preceding verses, which show that the believers' confidence came as a result of earlier experience. These Christians were not strangers to persecution, having encountered it soon after their conversion. It was then that they discovered the sufficiency of God's grace, and this gave birth to confidence in His faithfulness. Their confidence had sustained them in their previous sufferings and would see them through this one. Therefore, says the writer, don't cast it away; you are going to need it again.

Their confidence enabled them not only to endure shame and affliction, but to accept joyfully the seizure of their property. The key word is *joyfully*. A persecuted Christian may have no choice but to accept the loss of his possessions; but to accept it *joyfully* is another matter. They were able to do this "knowing that you have for yourselves a better possession and an abiding one." The experience taught them that, though the enemy might strip them of every earthly possession, their greatest possession, their wealth in Christ, could never be touched. Possessing nothing, they possessed everything. Loss of all worldly goods failed to diminish their assets. Bankrupt but rich, they were wealthy paupers.

And now it was happening again. As the angry waves of renewed persecution swept over them, the writer cried, "Remember! Remember the former days. Don't throw away your confidence. Remember!''

The exhortation to remember is one of the most frequent in the Bible. It is the watchword of faith. The past with its record of God's faithfulness is the Christian's greatest defense against encroaching discouragement. We preserve our confidence by remembering.

"I shall remember the deeds of the Lord; surely I will remember Thy wonders of old. I will meditate on all Thy work, and muse on Thy deeds" (Psalm 77:11, 12). Again and again, Israel, when cornered by catastrophe, believed its way to victory by recounting God's past mercies. Before he died, Moses rehearsed with the people all that God had done for the people and admonished them to remember.

Concerning the Lord's Supper, Christ said, "Do this in remembrance of Me" (1 Corinthians 11:24). Is it possible that we could forget that Jesus died for us? Evidently, it is. We may remember the fact of it but forget the force of it. We quickly forget the goodness of God. Unbelief has a short memory.

I recall more than one occasion when, having been delivered by God's grace at the eleventh hour, I declared, "I'll never doubt God again!" But in a few weeks—or days—when another seemingly impossible situation loomed on the horizon, I found myself cowering in the corner of self-pity, whimpering because God had abandoned me. Forgetfulness is definitely hazardous to your faith.

A BOOK OF REMEMBRANCES

Don't trust your memory. There's something about fallen human nature that finds it easy to forget spiritual things. We can remember a dirty joke we heard twenty years ago, but can't recall the preacher's text from last Sunday's sermon.

In 1970 I began keeping a record of answered prayers. For several years I faithfully jotted down in a little black book every specific answer, every instance of God's obvious mercy in times of trouble. Then I misplaced it and didn't recover it until two or three years later. I had moved my study from the church office to my home, and while unpacking a carton of books, I found it. How it got in the bottom of that box I'll never know—but there it was.

As I thumbed through it I was surprised to realize that I had forgotten most of the incidents mentioned. It was an opportune discovery, because at that time I was passing through a very trying period. To be honest, my faith was at an all-time low. But as I read through that little black book, something happened. My memory of God's wonderful faithfulness was revived and my sagging faith began to recover. By the time I read the last entry I was filled with rejoicing and *confidence*. Remembering had restored my confidence in the Lord.

There may come a time when you need to give your dying faith mouth-to-mouth resuscitation—and remembering is the best way to do it. Let me encourage you to start a Book of Remembrances. My Hebrew professor used to say, "Paper is cheaper than brains." You can find a good hardcover book filled with blank pages at most bookstores; or, if you prefer, a regular spiral notebook will do the trick. The important thing is to preserve a record of God's activity in your life. A chronicle of God's dealings and deliverances may someday mean the difference between victory and defeat.

His love in time past
Forbids me to think
He'll leave me at last
In trouble to sink;
Each sweet Ebenezar
I have in review,
Confirms His good pleasure
To help me quite through.

John Newton

WAITING FOR THE PROMISE INVOLVES OBEDIENCE TO GOD'S PRESENT WILL

"For you have need of endurance, so that when you have done the will of God, you may receive what was promised" (Hebrews 10:36).

Faith is not idle; it works while it waits. Receiving what God has promised requires obedience. We cannot expect God to fulfill His promise if we do not fulfill His will.

In the chapter, "How to Complete Your Faith," we discussed obedience as a part of faith—a distinctive act of obedience called for by a specific act of faith. Here the emphasis is upon continuing obedience to daily duty while we wait for God to respond to our faith.

It is significant that the writer, having exhorted his readers to cling to their confidence, makes no such appeal concerning obedience. If obedience is so important, why does he not here command them to obey? It is unnecessary.

Their obedience is assumed. Once confidence in the Lord has been established and firmly grounded, obedience will take care of itself. Obedience follows confidence as surely as thunder follows lightning. Even though it was obedience to God's will that got these people into trouble in the first place, God's past faithfulness had so clothed them with courageous confidence that they continued to obey regardless of the consequences. Only when confidence wavers does obedience hesitate.

WHEN THE UPRIGHT GET UPTIGHT

The Psalmist said, "Trust in the Lord, and do good" (Psalm 37:3). Here again confidence and obedience are linked together. This Psalm opens with a command to do the impossible: *"Fret not."* He is telling the upright not to get uptight. But there's so much to fret about! And it's so easy; it takes hardly any effort at all. But as usual, the Bible tells us how to do the impossible.

The alternative to fretfulness is given in verse 3: "Trust in the Lord, and do good." If we aren't careful we will see only the first familiar words, "Trust in the Lord," and barely notice the others: "and do good." Having committed the fretful situation to the Lord, trusting Him to handle it, we are to turn our attention to our everyday duty—doing good.

Doing good is proof we are trusting the Lord. If the trial through which we are passing so unsettles us as to prevent us from carrying on in everyday obedience, we have not truly trusted the matter to God. In a word, we have cast away our confidence.

Satan's strategy is to distract us from the will of God by paralyzing us with fear and anxiety. As a pastor I have seen believers incapacitated by worry to the extent that they could not function even in the simple details of daily living. But we have all felt that numbing preoccupation with a problem that drains the heart of all courage and concern; that awful lethargy that creeps over us because we have lost heart. The only effective counterattack is to trust the Lord. Trusting God to handle these fretful circumstances frees us to do His will without distraction. We overcome the evil by doing good.

I believe this is the point Christ makes in Matthew 6. He tells us not to be anxious for our life, what we shall eat or drink or wear, because our heavenly Father will see to it that we have all these things. Then comes the climax of the passage: "But seek first His kingdom and His righteousness; and all these things shall be added to you" (Matthew 6:33).

In other words, our concern is not to be with the physical and the material, but with the spiritual, with the kingdom of God and His righteousness. The point is, a person cannot seek *first* the things of God if his mind is preoccupied with the things of this world. It is the care of the world and the deceitfulness of riches (the mistaken belief that riches can erase the care of the world) that prevent the Word of God from bearing fruit in our hearts (Matthew 13:22).

Why does God promise to supply all our needs (Philippians 4:19)? Is it merely that we may have all we need? No, I think there is more to it than that. After all, even unbelievers have their needs supplied. Matter of fact, I know some unbelievers whose supply wagons carry much bigger loads than mine. Remember, while God is concerned about our physical life, His primary concern is with the spiritual. I believe the chief reason God promises to provide for our physical needs is so we can be free to seek Him and His kingdom. It works like this: If I don't have to worry about my life-needs, I can give my whole heart to seeking and serving Him.

Not long after graduating from seminary I was called to pastor a church in East Dallas. The former pastor had retired and remained a member of the church. In fact, it was he who recommended my name to the pulpit committee. A gracious and wise man, he later became a close friend and confidant. But when I was moving into the pastor's study he paid me a visit. He quietly told me that on his last Sunday as pastor of the church he had asked the church to take a certain action that would affect me.

"I hope you won't mind what I did," he said.

"What did you do?"

"I asked the church to increase your salary by seventy-five dollars a week."

"No," I said. "I don't mind. I don't mind at all. Not at all."

And then he said, "Now I didn't do that for you. I did it for this church."

"I don't think I understand," I said.

"Son," he said, "you can't do your best for the Lord or this church if you're having to worry about making ends meet. I want you to be free to give your best."

That was a wise man. And that is exactly what Jesus is saying in Matthew 6. God wants us free to concentrate all our heart-attention on His will and righteousness. And trusting our physical and material needs to God gives us that freedom.

Our confidence in God expresses itself by obedience. While we wait for the promise, we must keep our obedience up-to-date.

WAITING FOR THE PROMISE DEMANDS
PATIENCE FOR GOD'S FUTURE WORK

"For you have need of endurance, so that when you have done the will of God, you may receive what was promised" (Hebrews 10:36). The third condition for receiving the promise is endurance, or *patience*, as the word is often translated. Patience is the bridge between the doing of God's will and the receiving of the promise. Receiving what God has promised hinges not only upon doing God's will but on enduring after that will has been done. Many fail to receive because they fail to endure.

The writer is using the language of the athlete. A football team may be leading its opponents by one hundred points, but if the players quit before the final gun they will lose the game. The same is true with faith. We may be filled with courageous confidence, we may obey all God's will; but if we lack patience, we will lose the reward.

This patience, which Philo calls the "queen of virtues," is more than mere waiting or passive resignation. Barclay observes that "there is no single English word which transmits all the fullness of its meaning."[5] The Greek word literally means, "an abiding under," and contains the ideas of steadfastness, constancy, staying power. Another writer describes it as "a lively outgoing power of faith, and active energy."[6]

Ellicott says:

In this noble word there always appears a background of courage. It does not mark merely the endurance, but also the perseverance, the brave patience with which the Christian contends against the various hindrances, persecutions, and temptations that befall him in his conflict with the inward and outward world.[7]

This word is used most often in connection with trials. In classical Greek it was used of a plant's ability to live under hard and unfavorable circumstances.[8] If, as the writer to the Hebrews says, we *need* endurance, then we can expect to encounter difficulty. Mark it well: *faith never escapes testing.*

IS THIS TRIAL NECESSARY?

Somewhere along the way we picked up the idea that if a person commits his life to Christ and sincerely trusts the Lord, he will sail through life on calm seas. But both the Bible and our own experience testify that this is not the case. The apostle Peter wrote to early believers, "In this you greatly rejoice, even though now for a little while, *if necessary,* you have been distressed by various trials, that the proof of your faith, being more precious than gold which is perishable, even though tested by fire, may be found to result in praise and glory and honor at the revelation of Jesus Christ" (1 Peter 1:6, 7, emphasis mine).

Faith must be tested. An untried faith is an untrustworthy faith, because until it is put to the test we can never be sure if what we are calling faith is really faith. If there is a defect in our faith we need to know. That's why they test airplanes before they are mass-produced. And that's why test pilots are paid so well.

Not long ago, on our way to California, my family and I spent the night in Albuquerque, New Mexico. The next morning as I was loading our luggage into the trunk, a car came creeping through the parking lot and stopped beside me. A man and woman were inside and the man had a road map spread open over the steering wheel. He smiled and said hello and asked if I could help him. Assuming he was lost and wanted to ask directions, I went over to the car and told him I would be glad to if I could.

Suddenly he pulled his hand from under the road map and held up for my inspection a beautiful gold necklace.

"Like to buy a solid gold necklace cheap?" he said.

I glanced nervously over my shoulder, expecting to see police cars bearing down on us with lights flashing and sirens screaming. "Uh, no, thank you," I said, backing away. Why was I *thanking* him?

The necklace vanished and he jerked open his sport coat. "How about a genuine Rolex watch?" Pinned to the inside of his jacket was a wristwatch.

"No, thanks," I said and hauled myself out of there.

Back in the room, I told my wife what had happened, knowing she would share my indignation.

Which she did, of course. At first. Then, wistfully, she said, "You know, I'll bet we could have bought that necklace for next to nothing."

My wife is a great kidder.

But a person would be a fool to buy a necklace under those conditions. In the first place, it was probably so hot it smoked. And in the second place, all that glitters is not gold. The necklace could have been electroplated or only gold-plated. It would be stupid to buy it without having it tested.

All that glitters is not gold, and all that believes is not faith. And it is only by testing that we can determine the authenticity of our faith.

Also, it is by testing our faith that Christian character is produced (James 1:3, 4). And isn't that the real goal of our Christian experience—not that we might "get the blessing" but that our character be perfected? James tells us to count it all joy when we fall into various trials (James 1:2); but we can do that only if character means more to us than comfort.

RESIGNATION VS. ANTICIPATION

But there is another, perhaps more important, quality found in biblical patience: *expectation*. Biblical patience is not waiting with resignation but waiting with anticipation; it is waiting for something or someone. The word is often connected with some great and glorious goal. Barclay sums it up well:

It is not the patience which can sit down and bow its head and let things descend upon it and passively endure until the storm is past. . . . It is the spirit which can bear things, not simply with resignation, but with blazing hope; it is not the spirit which sits statically enduring in one place, but the spirit which bears things because it knows that these things are leading to a goal of glory; it is not patience which grimly waits for the end, but the patience which radiantly hopes for the dawn.[9]

The Psalmist tells us that waiting for the Lord is like waiting for the sunrise (Psalm 130:6). In waiting for the sunrise you can always count on two things: one, you can't rush it. Nothing you can do will hurry it; setting your clock ahead won't cause it to rise ahead of schedule. You must wait for it to rise in its own time. Two, the sun *does* rise. It always has and it always will. Those who wait for the morning are never disappointed. Neither are those who wait for the Lord.

Patient endurance—it even *sounds* awful; it sounds grim and cheerless and foreboding. Few things in life are more unappealing, more agonizing, more maddening, than waiting. How is it possible to stand calmly on the deck of a storm-battered ship and wait patiently for God to still the tempest?

It is the element of *anticipation* that makes such patient endurance possible. And that is what the author of Hebrews is speaking of in verse 37:

FOR YET IN A VERY LITTLE WHILE, HE WHO IS COMING WILL COME, AND WILL NOT DELAY.

This is a quotation from Habakkuk 2:3. There the people were waiting for God to destroy the Chaldeans who were laying siege to the city and threatening them with destruction. The prophecy opens with Habakkuk's complaint that his repeated cries to the Lord for help have gone unanswered. Now in the second chapter God speaks in answer to the prophet's complaint. The purpose and promise of God will be fulfilled, the Lord says. Even though it appears to linger, it will be fulfilled in its due time.

The writer of Hebrews takes up the theme and applies it to the present situation. "He who is coming will come, and will not delay." It may look like delay to those waiting, but the Lord is right on schedule.

The phrase, "He who is coming," is literally, "the Coming One," the participle indicating character; that is His constant attitude, not an occasional activity. In other words, His coming is more than a response to their prayers; it is a response to His character. Not to come in deliverance and promise would be to deny His own nature. He is always coming; He is ever the Coming One. We could say, He is always *in transit*.

IT'S IN THE AIR

In 1975 I resigned the pastorate to enter a full-time traveling ministry. Knowing ahead of time that I would do this, the Lord caused the country's largest airport, the Dallas/Ft. Worth Regional Airport, to be built within two miles of my house just so it would be convenient for my wife, Kaye, to meet my late-night flights (not many people are aware of this).

A few years ago I was flying home from a conference up north, scheduled to arrive on Flight 214 at midnight. Kaye arrived a few minutes before twelve and went to the gate to meet me. Twelve o'clock came but the plane didn't. Nothing unusual about that, so she waited. But after a while she went to the ticket counter and asked the agent when they expected Flight 214.

"In about thirty minutes," the agent said.

Kaye decided to wait in the car and listen to the radio. Thirty minutes later she returned to the gate but the flight still hadn't arrived. She went back to the ticket counter. "Any word on Flight 214?"

"Looks like another thirty minutes, at least."

Another thirty minutes dragged by. With the exception of the few people waiting to meet Flight 214, the terminal was practically deserted.

"It's me again. Look, don't you know when 214's going to be here?"

The agent looked up from the stack of papers he was sorting. "I'm sorry, but we do not have that information. Check back later."

Puzzled, my wife wandered around the terminal waiting for a decent interval to pass when she could go back to the ticket counter.

"Excuse me," she said, "but you must have some idea when the plane is going to be here."

Again the agent stopped what he was doing and looked at

her without smiling. "I'm sorry, ma'am, but we do not have that information."

"Well," she insisted, "at least you can tell me what time it left!"

"I'm sorry, but we do not have that information. If you would check back in a few minutes. . . ."

She couldn't understand the agent's strange behavior and why it had changed so suddenly. Surely they knew what time a flight took off; no big mystery about that. Why not tell her? Unless. . . . And then it hit her. She rushed back to the ticket counter, with visions of crashed and burning planes in her head.

"Listen!" she said to the agent. "About Flight 214! I don't want to know when it left. I don't want to know when it's going to get here. But can you tell me just one thing? *Is it in the air?*"

The agent smiled and said, "Yes, it's in the air."

"Thank you. That's all I need to know."

And the rest of the waiting was easy. She could wait with patience, knowing it was in the air.

And there have been times in my life, times of unexplained trials and unrelieved heartaches, when I have come to the Lord and asked, "Lord, why?" and the answer has been, "I'm sorry, but I can't give you that information."

"Lord," I have cried, "how long? When will You deliver me from all this?"

"I'm sorry, but I can't give you that information."

And in desperation, I have cried, "Lord, can You tell me just this much: not when You will end this or how You will end it. But just this: Is it in the air?"

And the Lord has said, "Yes, child, it is in the air."

And that has been enough. I can wait patiently for the Lord because I know He *is* coming; He is always coming. He is on the way. It is in the air.

Thus far we prove that promise good,
Which Jesus ratified with blood.
Still He is faithful, wise and just,
And still in Him believers trust.

NOTES

1. Eric Hoffer, *The Temper of Our Time* (New York: Harper & Row, Publishers, 1967), p. 120.
2. J. Sidlow Baxter, *Does God Still Guide?* (Grand Rapids: Zondervan Publishing House, 1968), p. 155.
3. Edwin and Lillian Harvey, *Kneeling We Triumph* (Chicago: Moody Press, 1974), p. 31.
4. C. S. Lewis, *The Best of C. S. Lewis* (Grand Rapids: Baker Book House, 1969), p. 513.
5. William Barclay, *A New Testament Wordbook* (London: SCM Press, 1955), p. 59.
6. Alan Richardson, ed., *A Theological Wordbook of the Bible* (New York: The Macmillan Company, 1960), p. 165. Copyright © 1950, and renewed 1978, by Macmillan Publishing Co., Inc.
7. C. Leslie Mitton, *The Epistle of James* (Grand Rapids: Wm. B. Eerdmans Publishing Co., 1966), p. 23.
8. Barclay, p. 59.
9. *Ibid.*, p. 60.

CHAPTER TWELVE
A Final Word — How Faith Grows

God allows us to set the level and the limit of our own blessings. In a very real sense, we determine the extent to which God uses or blesses us. When we pray, as we often do, "Lord, bless me more," I think I can hear the Lord reply, "Child, I'm blessing you now all you will let me."

Let's look at some Scripture passages:

"Give, and it will be given to you; good measure, pressed down, shaken together, running over, they will pour into your lap. *For whatever measure you deal out to others, it will be dealt to you in return*" (Luke 6:38, emphasis added).

"For in the way you judge, you will be judged; *and by your standard of measure, it shall be measured to you*" (Matthew 7:2, emphasis added).

"And He was saying to them, 'Take care what you listen to. *By your standard of measure it shall be measured to you*; and more shall be given you besides' " (Mark 4:24, emphasis added).

Matthew records the incident of two blind men following Jesus, begging Him to heal them: "And after He had come into the house, the blind men came up to Him, and Jesus said to them, 'Do you believe that I am able to do this?' They said to Him, 'Yes, Lord.' Then He touched their eyes, saying, '*Be it done to you according to your faith,* ' " (Matthew 9:28, 29, emphasis added).

An excellent illustration of this principle is found in 2 Kings 4, the story of the widow and the pot of oil. The woman's husband had died, leaving her two children and an unpaid debt, and the creditor planned to make slaves of her sons. When she turned to Elisha for help, the prophet asked what she had in her house. Evidently, he had in mind staging the first garage sale in history. Anyway, she told him she had nothing in the house except a pot of oil, hardly worth mentioning.

The prophet instructed her to gather all the empty vessels she could and fill them from the one jar of oil; then she could sell the oil, pay off the creditor, and save her sons. Without any hesitation, the woman obeyed the outlandish words of this strange prophet. And the miracle happened. But notice what occurred in verse 6: "And it came about when the vessels were full, that she said to her son, 'Bring me another vessel.' And he said to her, 'There is not one vessel more.' *And the oil stopped*" (emphasis added).

The oil stopped. As long as there was room to receive it, the oil poured forth. The flow of the oil was determined, not by God's ability to give it, but by the woman's capacity to receive it. If, when the flow stopped, the woman had prayed, "Lord, give me more oil," I am certain the Lord would have said, "Woman, give me more vessels!"

Many folks are praying for more oil when they ought to be gathering more vessels. If we are spiritually impoverished, it is not because the hand of grace is tight-fisted; it is because the hand of faith is too weak. The hand of faith is smaller than the hand of grace.

A few years ago a supermarket staged a contest in which the winner was allowed to plunge his hands into a barrel filled with silver dollars, keeping all his hands could hold. As the winner leered at the barrel of glittering silver dollars, he said, "I wish I had bigger hands."

F. B. Meyer said, "If only a soul can believe in God, to
the extent to which it believes it can obtain anything that is in
the heart of God to bestow."[1] If the law of the Christian life
is "according to your faith," then it is vital that our faith grow.

DIFFERING DEGREES OF FAITH

In chapter three I stated that with faith the main thing is the
object of faith and not its size. But that is not to say that size
is unimportant. Jesus rebuked little faith (Matthew 6:30; 8:26;
14:31; 16:8) and commended great faith (Matthew 8:10;
15:28).

That faith can and should grow is evident from the use of
such phrases as "little faith" and "great faith." Paul looked
forward to the increase of the Corinthians' faith (2 Corinthians
10:15). He longed to go to Thessalonica to complete what was
lacking in the faith of the believers there (1 Thessalonians
3:10); and in his second letter to them he wrote of their faith
enlarging (2 Thessalonians 1:3). In Romans 1:17, Paul em-
ploys the phrase, "from faith to faith," which Charles B.
Williams translates, "the way of faith that leads to greater
faith."

The book of Acts speaks of certain men as being "full of
faith" (Acts 6:5, 8; 11:24). This phrase seems to indicate a
habitual characteristic as opposed to an occasional activity.
What was an exception in some had become the rule in others.
All Christians experience the periodic gift of faith during times
of extremity. But there is a vast difference between these in-
termittent acts of faith, "emergency rations," as it were, and
the continuing, day-by-day posture of faith. It is the difference
between scraping the bottom of the barrel for a crumb of faith
and a constant resting in an abundant supply. To one, faith is
a last resort; to the other it is the first response.

Paul describes Abraham as growing strong in faith (Romans
4:20). As we have seen, Abraham's faith is the standard for
all believers. Using him as our example, we may say that
strong faith is (1) *believing before the fact*; that is, believing

when there is nothing to base our faith upon except the bare Word of God; and (2) *believing in spite of the facts*; that is, believing when outward circumstances contradict everything God has said.

John White defines great faith in this way: "Great faith is responding to God when it is hardest to do so, either when the thing he demands of you hurts or else seems totally impractical . . . it is faith that continues to respond to the Word of God in the absence of outward encouragement."[2]

We are strong or great in faith when the first and natural response to crisis or need is trust. It is trusting God by choice rather than by circumstance or force.

HOW FAITH GROWS

Basically God uses two cooperating methods to increase our faith: knowledge and experience.

1. Knowledge

Knowledge of God Himself. Remember the word of the Psalmist: "And those who know thy name will put their trust in Thee" (Psalm 9:10). The name of God is God—as He has revealed Himself to us, His nature, His character, His purpose. Having discussed this in earlier chapters, suffice it to say that faith grows in much the same way it was born—as it looks unto Jesus.

Knowledge of God's Word. "Faith comes from hearing, and hearing by the word of Christ" (Romans 10:17). Spurgeon said, "The sight of the promises themselves is good for the eyes of faith: the more we study the words of grace, the more grace shall we derive from the words."[3] The Word of God planted in the heart becomes a seed that will inevitably blossom, when watered with obedience, into a striking flower of faith. Your faith will grow in direct proportion to your knowledge of and commitment to the Word.

*How firm a foundation, ye saints of the Lord,
Is laid for your faith in His excellent Word!*

What more can He say than to you He hath said,
To you who for refuge to Jesus have fled?

Knowledge of God's works. By this, I mean the testimonies of others. It was the testimony of the Samaritan woman that drew all the men of her village out to see and hear Jesus. And remember, the witnesses of Hebrews 11 are not "spectator witnesses" but "testifying witnesses." My own faith was greatly helped by reading the story of J. Hudson Taylor in *Hudson Taylor's Spiritual Secret*. Read the biographies of men and women who knew what it meant to trust God; they are nourishing food for a growing faith.

2. *Experience*

I have two statements to make:

Statement #1: We learn to trust God by trusting God.

We do not learn to trust God by listening to sermons on trusting God or by reading books on faith (even this one). We learn to trust by trusting. As we exercise what faith we have, it grows and develops into a stronger, healthier faith. It is by experience that we discover God can really be trusted after all, and that He does keep His promises.

When David was trying to persuade Saul to let him have a crack at Goliath, the lad was almost cocky in his belief that God would be with him. But he had good reason to be. God had already proved Himself faithful by enabling David to slay a lion and a bear that attacked the flock he had been tending. "The Lord who delivered me from the paw of the lion and from the paw of the bear, He will deliver me from the hand of this Philistine" (1 Samuel 17:37).

I thank God for the mountains
And I thank Him for the valleys,
I thank Him for the storms He brought me through,
For if I'd never had a problem
I wouldn't know that He could solve them,
I'd never know what faith in God could do.[4]

We sometimes sing a little chorus that says, "Jesus is all I need." That's true, but we'll never know He is all we need until He is all we've got.

Statement #2: We will not trust God until we have to.

There is something about fallen human nature that finds it terribly difficult to "lean not unto our own understanding" and to trust in the Lord. As long as we have one more trick up our sleeve, one more gimmick in our hand, one more dollar in the bank, we'll not trust God. I know there are exceptions, but that's exactly what they are—exceptions.

But if we only learn to trust by trusting, and if we will not trust until we have to, then God must see to it that we have to.

The old saints used to have a phrase we would do well to revive: to be *shut up to faith*. Being shut up to faith meant being in a situation in which there was no choice but to trust God. The only way out was up. Having closed off every other avenue of escape, God had them shut up to faith. Other options were swept away. Like it or not, it was sink or swim, trust God or perish.

Israel at the Red Sea, for instance. That's a classic example of how God shuts us up to faith. With the mountains on either side and all the Egyptians in the world swooping down from behind, only *forward* was left. And forward was the Red Sea. And that's what God told them to do: Go forward—into the Red Sea. And they did. It was either trust God or be delivered again into bondage. But do you think they would have moved an inch in the direction of the Red Sea had not the Egyptians been behind them, forcing them to do so? Not on your life.

Understanding this "way of God" will unravel a lot of mysteries and explain a lot of pressure-cooker situations in which we have found ourselves. Often God is simply shutting us up to faith.

A number of years ago I read the biography of George Mueller, that great saint of Bristol, who for years supported a large orphanage by nothing but prayer and faith. The stories of his great faith set a fire in my heart. I longed to be able to trust God like that. I remember kneeling one day in my study and praying earnestly that God would teach me to live by faith. I guess I thought God would wave a wand over my head, put a holy zap on me, and suddenly I would be a giant of faith, waiting for a vacancy in Hebrews 11. Instead, everything came unglued. Financial problems, ministerial difficulties, family crises—somebody was definitely out to get me. I went to my knees, begging God to help me, asking what was happening and why.

"I'm just answering your prayer," He seemed to say.

"Prayer? What prayer? I don't remember praying for disaster."

"Your prayer for faith," He said.

Later I came across this piece by an unknown author.

THE LORD'S WAY

I asked the Lord that I might grow
In faith and love and every grace —
Might more of His salvation know,
And seek more earnestly His face.

'Twas He who taught me thus to pray,
And He, I trust, has answered prayer;
But it has been in such a way
As almost drove me to despair.

I hoped that in some favored hour
At once He'd answer my request;
And, by His love's consuming power,
Subdue my sins, and give me rest.

Instead of this, He made me feel
The hidden evils of my heart,
And let the angry powers of hell
Assault my soul in every part.

Yes, more, with His own hand He seemed
Intent to aggravate my woe;

Crossed all the fair designs I schemed,
Blasted my gourds, and laid them low.

"Lord, why is this?" I trembling cried:
"Wilt Thou pursue Thy worm to death?"
"'Tis in this way," the Lord replied,
"I answer prayer for grace and faith.

"These inward trials I employ,
From self and pride to set thee free
And break the schemes of earthly joy,
That thou mayest seek thy all in Me."

God's greatest and toughest task is teaching us to trust Him, for without faith it is impossible to please Him. And He will do whatever is necessary to enroll us in that school from which there is no graduation.

NOTES

1. F. B. Meyer, *Through Fire and Blood* (New York: Fleming H. Revell, 1896), p. 10.
2. John White, *The Fight* (Downers Grove: InterVarsity Press, 1976), pp. 102, 103.
3. C. H. Spurgeon, *Faith's Checkbook* (Chicago: Moody Press, n.d.), p. ii.
4. *Through It All*, Words and music by Andraé Crouch, published by Manna Music, Inc., Burbank, California, 1971.